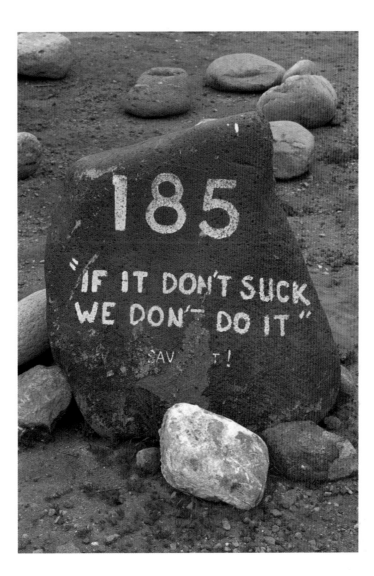

TO BE A U.S. NAVY SEAL

Cliff Hollenbeck &

Dick Couch

ZENITH
PRESS

For Tommy Norris

Special thanks to the officers and men of Naval Special Warfare Command, who give so much so that all of us may enjoy the blessings of freedom and the American way of life. This is especially true of Tommy Norris: Medal of Honor recipient, retired naval officer, SEAL (Class 45), retired FBI agent, and friend, to whom this book is dedicated.

First published in 2003 by MBI Publishing Company and Zenith Press, an imprint of MBI Publishing Company, 400 1st Avenue North, Suite 300, Minneapolis, MN 55401 USA

Zenith Press titles are also available at discounts in bulk quantity for industrial or sales-promotional use. For details write to Special Sales Manager at MBI Publishing Company, 400 1st Avenue North, Suite 300, Minneapolis, MN 55401 USA.

To find out more about our books, join us online at www.zenithpress.com.

Library of Congress Cataloging-in-Publication Data
Hollenbeck, Cliff
    To Be a U.S. Navy SEAL/by Cliff Hollenbeck.
        p. cm.
    ISBN 978-0-7603-1404-3 (pbk. : alk. paper)
        1. United States. Navy. SEALs. 2. United States. Navy—Commando troops. I. Title.

VG87.H65 2003
359.9'84—dc21   2003041261

Edited by Leah Cochenet Noel
Designed by Mandy Iverson
Printed in Singapore

On the front cover: The entire Basic Underwater Demolition/SEAL (BUD/S) class waits for instructions at the pool's side. All the men, who now have entered phase two of training, have completed their basic scuba instruction and will complete a simple swim-in-gear session. This is done to help build physical stamina for their long, open-ocean underwater swims. While there is no pass or fail for this portion of the phase, competition to be first is fierce among the teams. As always, the last-place team has to do pushups in full dive gear.

On the back cover (top): Future U.S. Navy SEALs are attacked underwater in simulated-combat situations. Instructors pull masks, fins, and breathing regulators off their students, who must recover the equipment and continue the swim test. As with all proficiency tests, the trainees must pass this stage of training in order to progress to the more advanced classes of open-ocean scuba diving. **(bottom):** A group of trainees run along the beach sporting the true look of a SEAL hopeful: wet and full of sand. Often, as a form of punishment, the trainees are sent into the surf to dunk themselves in water and then are ordered to roll in the beach sand before returning to training exercises.

On the frontispiece: Each BUD/S class leaves a little memento or sign behind for future classes in the program. By the time new trainees see this rock on San Clemente Island, they have a good idea how the saying was reached. Trainees take and obey endless commands to perform physical and mental exercises. Many of those exercises seem without much value except to intimidate or harass. In fact, every exercise a trainee completes is in preparation to meet the challenges experienced by SEALs in combat.

On the title page: SEAL team training Class 228 paddles through the rolling surf near San Diego, competing to see which team will be first. Most of the teams are content to keep their small craft from capsizing into the cold water. The crew finishing first will get a nice rest, while the last-place boat crew will make another trip into the surf.

On contents page: A U.S. Navy SEAL team operator is dressed in camouflage in preparation for a counterterrorism attack. SEAL team operators train extensively in advanced forms of armed and unarmed hand-to-hand fighting. Each item of clothing and equipment that has been introduced to them in BUD/S and tactical training will be part of the basic gear throughout their attachment with the SEAL teams.

CONTENTS

THE PHOTOGRAPHY

Very little in the worlds of photography or journalism can accurately capture the hours upon hours of freezing cold, strained muscles, numbing exhaustion, and mental fatigue faced in training by young men aspiring to become Navy SEALs. When you see or read about a trainee being "wet and sandy," it's difficult to imagine what it feels like to start every day, for several months, in this condition. Through my photos and Dick Couch's words, we hope to share some of the challenges faced by these exceptional men.

In order to photograph Navy SEAL training, the photographer has to be where the training is conducted and be there when the training is conducted. Rarely is this training done under conditions photographers would call ideal or beautiful. The harsh glare of a hot sun at noon, baking a trainee doing pushups in the dirt; the cold ocean surf spilling over a team in its rubber boat; the countless hours working under cold water; and the dirt and grime covering everything and everyone during a long run down the beach—to a SEAL these are some of the foundations of his world. To these men, this environment is their life. And, for the better part of two years, it also became a challenge for my camera.

More than 100 exceptionally physically fit and mentally prepared men stood ready for their first day of training to begin. Every man had obviously spent months in preparation for this day. Each looked like a possible graduate. As readers will learn, less than 15 percent of the average class completes SEAL team training. My challenge was to photograph every step a candidate must complete to become a Navy SEAL. I made several thousand photos showing every man in every phase of training. As their numbers became smaller, it became more obvious who would still be there at graduation. While the photography process was easy, as the photographs show, the training itself never became easy.

The Navy's Special Warfare Command gave Dick Couch and me complete access to all phases of SEAL basic training. We were allowed to watch, photograph, and, in some cases, participate in anything we chose. Dick made many of the long day and night beach runs. I did several underwater training sessions with a camera. Neither of us did pushups in the wet sand, although Dick can easily do 50 without breaking a sweat. We were not allowed to interfere with training, so there were few opportunities to pose photos. Now and then a trainee would mug the camera with a smile or funny act, usually earning the entire class 20 pushups. Those pushups were never a deterrent to their antics.

The generous accommodation by the Navy has helped us present one of the most accurate representations of this often fictionalized training. Our unprecedented access came primarily as a result of Dick's longevity as a member and reserve commanding officer of that elite group, his status as a decorated combat veteran, and the positive portrayal he gives SEALs in his best-selling novels. Anyone wishing an accurate story or two about Navy SEALs in action needs to look no further than his well-crafted novels.

No special photographic equipment was used to make photographs for this book. Nikon 35mm land and underwater cameras and lenses and Kodak medium- and high-speed films were used for every photo. The resulting negatives were scanned to Kodak professional photo discs for separation and placement by the publisher.

It has been interesting, educational, and, at times, exciting to follow these future SEALs through their Basic Underwater Demolition/SEAL (BUD/S) training. It also has been a privilege meeting dedicated young men who, a few months later, have laid their lives on the line for their country, for little pay or personal recognition. I especially appreciate working with Dick Couch, my friend, a true warrior, and one of the best and most knowledgeable military authors in the business. It was a lot of fun watching and photographing some of the things we did as younger men—a lot easier too, as Dick pointed out many times during this project.

I would like to thank every member of the Special Warfare Command, especially the BUD/S instructors, who made things easy for us. I would also like to thank Dick for inviting me along on his special warfare projects, which in turn allowed me to relive a few moments of my own youth. Making pictures along the Silver Strand, swimming in the combat pool, hiking on San Clemente Island, visiting the various clubs, staying at the bachelor officers' quarters, and simply wandering around the naval amphibious base and Coronado, California, all these years later were enjoyable experiences I'll never forget. Something I had forgotten is the esprit de corps and camaraderie of the gentlemen whom we have serving in our military forces, especially considering what we ask and train them to do for our nation. I was treated with a degree of courtesy and respect not often found in the outside world.

—Cliff Hollenbeck

SEAL team operators stand ready to undertake military actions, as their name implies—on the sea, in the air, and on the land. They are an exclusive unit within the military's umbrella of special forces. While their numbers are small, their mission and history are not. Membership into this elite group begins with the completion of BUD/S, Basic Underwater Demolition/SEAL training, conducted at the Naval Amphibious Base Coronado in Coronado, California.

Navy SEAL teams are a very exclusive club. It is a closed society for warriors, and the price of admission is steep. Basic Underwater Demolition/ SEAL (BUD/S) training is the crucible through which every man who hopes to become a Navy SEAL must pass. Getting through BUD/S does not make a Navy SEAL, but all SEALs must successfully complete BUD/S. This 27-week SEAL basic school graduates fewer than 250 men each year, and not all of them will become SEALs. BUD/S graduates must complete another intensive 15 weeks of advanced training to qualify as SEALs. Only then are they awarded their SEAL pin, called a trident. Throw in the basic SEAL indoctrination course and Army Airborne training, and it takes about a year to earn the title Navy SEAL. Then the "new guys" face another 18 months of difficult and demanding training before they are ready for their first SEAL deployment.

SEAL training is unique. It is designed to find men who have the heart and the talent to become warriors. The traditional military services train men and women together. The idea is that they will serve together during their military careers and should therefore train together, beginning with boot camp. There are women attached to the SEAL teams, but they serve only in support roles. Female Navy SEALs are found only in the movies.

All services train their officers and enlisted personnel separately during their basic warfare instruction. In BUD/S, officers and enlisted men train and suffer together, side by side. BUD/S training is the glue that binds all SEALs together, from seaman to admiral. There are a number of "wannabes" who claim to be Navy SEALs. Most claim that they joined the SEAL teams from another special operations unit or received some exotic clandestine training. There is only one way into the SEAL teams and that is through BUD/S. A Navy SEAL will always tell you his class. In my case, I was Class 45. Cliff, while not a SEAL team

operator, completed dive and jump training with Class 34 and weapons and tactics training with Class 35. His BUD/S training was the same as hospital corpsmen of that era who served in the teams, and we are proud to call them fellow SEALs.

The first SEAL teams were commissioned in 1962, just in time for the Vietnam War. The early character of the SEALs was formed in that conflict. Forty-two SEALs were killed in action in Vietnam. Cliff and I personally knew and served with many of them. I have been to The Wall and seen their names in that place of honor. Since Vietnam, SEALs have fought in every skirmish and near-war that has touched our nation. They have died fighting Al Qaeda terrorists in the mountains of Afghanistan. Navy SEALs are fully committed to the war on terrorism. As long as the followers of Osama bin Laden and Al Qaeda threaten America, Navy SEALs will stand in harm's way to oppose them.

SEAL training, beginning from day one at BUD/S, is designed to create warriors, modern American samurai. It is a sorting process that finds young men who would rather die than quit, then instills in them a relentless desire to fight and win as a team. Once a prospective SEAL trainee reports for BUD/S training, he is immediately immersed in the culture of the SEAL teams. It is a tradition-bound ritual, but one that is sensitive to the changes needed as the role of the warrior evolves in the modern era. But as you will see in this visual journey of SEAL training, it is a dirty, difficult, and dangerous business. In secret terrorist training camps in Africa and the Middle East, the forces of evil are priming their young men for war. They are a formidable enemy, so our warriors must be superior to them in every way. They must be not only physically and technically dominant, but morally superior as well.

BUD/S trainees learn early on that they have a sacred duty as American warriors to the nation they serve and to the SEAL warriors who have gone before them. Navy SEAL training is physically demanding, but it is also about honor, courage, commitment, accountability, reliability, and personal integrity. A Navy SEAL warrior also must be hard from the inside out.

BUD/S is just the beginning of a young man's journey to become a warrior. Today, it takes more than 30 months to train a Navy SEAL and prepare him for combat. At that point, he is certified and ready for deployment—an apprentice warrior in the SEAL trade and still a "new guy" in his platoon. When he comes back from his first deployment, he is called a "one-tour wonder" and is no more than a journeyman in the trade.

As SEAL training has become longer and more comprehensive in recent years, one aspect of this training has remained the same: In order to get one good man, begin with five good men. Since the birth of the Navy frogmen at Fort Pierce during World War II, this forging of warriors through adversity and attrition has always been unlike any military training in the world. In this ruthless process, for every man who succeeds, four men will fail. It's a rendering for men of character, spirit, and a burning desire to win at all costs. It is a unique and often brutal rite of passage that forms the basis of this distinctive warrior culture.

To examine SEAL training today, the Navy allowed Cliff and me to follow BUD/S Class 228 from day one to graduation. It was an opportunity for us to journey back in time, to revisit this very difficult training and the very special culture. Sometimes, when the men in

Class 228 were sent for repeated trips into the cold surf or were bound hand and foot and tossed into the pool, we would both react as if the pain were ours, and as if we were the men still in the arena. Even after all this time has passed, we still share their scar tissue. In this book, you're going to meet the young men who want to be SEALs. You are going to share their journey and join this elite band of warriors, through my words and the eyes of Cliff Hollenbeck.

I have known Cliff Hollenbeck for more than 15 years, but we go back much further. We are both from the Vietnam generation of warriors. I saw Vietnam from the land and sea through a gun sight. Cliff saw Vietnam from the land and from the air and through the lens of a camera. He is a decorated combat veteran. When I was asked to tell the story of modern SEAL training with Class 228, I knew words alone would be inadequate. I immediately called Cliff. His images graced the picture section of our book *The Warrior Elite*, but the full-color, illustrated measure of the struggle and suffering of Class 228 is found in these pages.

Cliff Hollenbeck is an award-winning photojournalist, film producer, composer, and acclaimed author in his own right. One has only to listen to *Songi di Amore,* a CD collection of Italian arias written and produced by Cliff, to know that he has the soul of a poet. If a picture is worth a thousand words, then the blood, sweat, and toil of SEAL training is easily worth 10 of my books. I am proud to call Cliff Hollenbeck a friend, collaborator, and fellow warrior.

—Dick Couch

Trainees in Basic Underwater Demolition/ SEAL (BUD/S) training spend most of their first few weeks wet, cold, and sandy. While a good photograph can show the wet and grime, nothing can truly illustrate how miserable this feels day in and day out for six months. When a class hasn't performed as the instructor wishes, he commands the trainees to "hit the surf." Often as not, a class gets that command even when it performs well.

CHAPTER 1
INDOCTRINATION:

After a drill procedure mistake is made, this boat crew drops for a wet and dirty 20 pushups during the indoctrination course. A beautiful set of condominiums overlooks the beach in the distance, but none of the boat crews dares look in that direction. Their attention is on the instructor. But lots of mistakes are made during this early stage of Basic Underwater Demolition/SEAL (BUD/S) training, and another crew must drop.

'HOO-YAH'

Potential SEALs shiver in the cold early-morning light, waiting for their training to begin. It will start with a splash, as they hit the combat pool. Trainees must swim well just to get into the BUD/S training program. During the next few months, they will spend many hours in the water, learning some well-tested swimming techniques. Eventually, they will be able to endure long hours in, and under, the water. By graduation, and for the rest of their lives, they will consider the water a second home.

Basic Underwater Demolition/SEAL (BUD/S) training begins for Class 228 early on an October morning. The place is on the naval amphibious base in Coronado, California. The base is still quiet. Behind a chain-link fence with diagonal privacy slats, Class 228 waits anxiously on the concrete pool deck of the naval special warfare combat training tank (CTT). The new BUD/S trainees wear only canvas underwater demolition team (UDT) swim trunks. They are compressed into tight rows, chest to back, in bobsled fashion to conserve body heat. They are wet from a recent shower. Neat rows of duffle bags that contain the students' uniforms, boots, and training gear separate

each human file. The students had arrived 30 minutes earlier to roll and stow the pool covers and string the lane markers. The first day of training has begun.

BUD/S training is conducted in three distinct phases. First Phase is the conditioning phase, followed by Second Phase—diving—and Third Phase—weapons and tactics. In order to prepare themselves for the rigors of First Phase training, the trainees must first complete several weeks of preparation called the indoctrination course. For Class 228, the indoctrination course, or Indoc, will last two weeks. In it they will learn the rules and conventions of BUD/S training. They will learn how to conduct themselves at the pool,

Simple and basic physical training exercises on the smooth sand of Coronado's Silver Strand start each morning of a trainee's life. Within the first hour of exercise, each will have done more than 100 pushups, equally split between other exercises. Instructors are among the best active-duty SEALs. They lead and demonstrate every exercise, usually without breathing hard. By the time First Phase is completed, the trainees who remain will be in similar physical shape.

Sitting in tight rows, chest to back, trainees conserve their body heat after many hours of indoctrination in the combat pool. The volunteers accepted into training have spent weeks prior to this program physically preparing themselves for the demands of SEAL training. Every man sitting in this group has the physical look and promise to become a SEAL. But when the class finally graduates, only one in 10 will have withstood the demanding training.

An instructor stresses the importance of training and working as a team, be it two men or 100. This is especially important when the class works in the pool or in open water. If one man gets tired during a long swim, it's up to his swim buddy to help. If one man drifts farther than an arm's reach from his swim buddy, the whole class drops for 20 pushups as punishment.

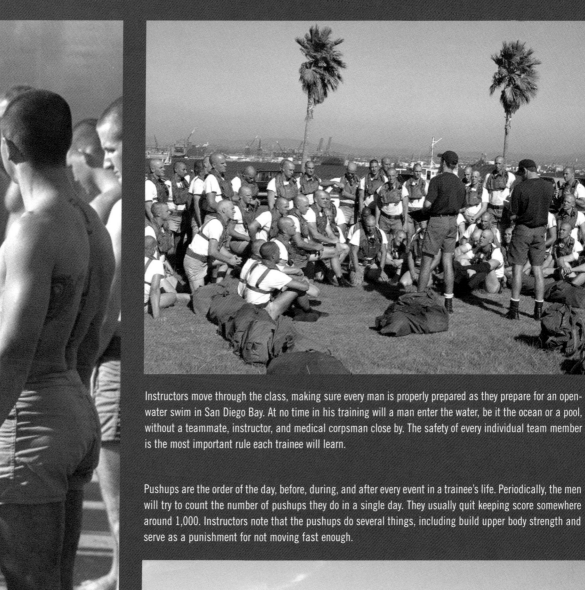

Instructors move through the class, making sure every man is properly prepared as they prepare for an open-water swim in San Diego Bay. At no time in his training will a man enter the water, be it the ocean or a pool, without a teammate, instructor, and medical corpsman close by. The safety of every individual team member is the most important rule each trainee will learn.

Pushups are the order of the day, before, during, and after every event in a trainee's life. Periodically, the men will try to count the number of pushups they do in a single day. They usually quit keeping score somewhere around 1,000. Instructors note that the pushups do several things, including build upper body strength and serve as a punishment for not moving fast enough.

Trainees return from a four-mile run along the Silver Strand Beach. In the afternoon, the run is hot and dusty, changed only by the occasional trip into the surf and roll in the burning, rough sand. Every run is timed and every man is expected to improve. If the class is slower than the week before, everyone gets a little extra running and another trip into the surf. The competition to be first is fierce because the winner usually gets to rest, while the others get wet, sandy, and more miserable.

No BUD/S trainee walks anywhere—ever. They must run as a pair, or a class, to breakfast, to lunch, to dinner, and to every event during a day's training. They have to ask permission to leave any session, even to go to the bathroom, and they must be running within a step or two. Most of the men even run during their rare off hours. Running becomes their only way of getting from one point to the next. It's just another way of separating the men from the boys.

Morning physical training starts with stretching exercises. While this is an easy warmup, the hour-long program will try to test and strengthen every muscle in a trainee's body. By the end of the hour, every man will have made at least one trip into the cold surf, followed by a roll in the hot sand.

how to run the obstacle course, and how to maneuver small boats through the surf. They also will learn the complex set of procedures and protocols needed in First Phase and the rest of BUD/S training, customs they must observe if they hope to survive this rite of passage. During this indoctrination period, they also begin to learn about SEAL culture, the ethos of this warrior class.

At any time during Indoc, BUD/S officers and senior petty officers in training may be asked, "How many men do you have?" The trainee leader had better have a good count and know where his men are. If he does not, the consequences are harsh and immediate. SEALs have died in combat, but never has one been left behind. A SEAL leader must always be able to account for his men.

Indoc also helps the trainees prepare physically for First Phase. Many of the training evolutions in Indoc are the same as those in First Phase. But in First Phase, they will be conducted with much more rigor and intensity. These weeks of indoctrination are designed to bring the class together physically and mentally. This is a very important time. Most of the students have prepared for this individually. Now they will live and train as a class, as a team.

One hundred fourteen souls were originally assigned, or had orders, to BUD/S Class 228. Most are relatively new to the Phil H. Bucklew Naval

When regular pushups become routine, instructors order trainees to push their IBS (inflatable boat, small) up over their heads and hold it for a while. Eventually the crewmen's arms get tired and the boat sinks to their heads and shoulders. Then it's time to hit the surf with their boat, often filling it with water and bringing it back for some additional lifts. If the crew is one man short, too bad.

Special Warfare Center in Coronado, California, where BUD/S is conducted. Of those 114 men who thought they wanted to become Navy SEALs, only 98 are on the roster on the first day of indoctrination. Young sailors drop out for any number of reasons, but many are simply intimidated. When they see what SEAL trainees are asked to do, they quit before they begin. So the attrition began even before Class 228 started its first official day of training. Any student at BUD/S, at any time, can drop on request (DOR). All he has to do is say, "I quit." Those assigned to Class 228 who quit prior to the beginning of indoctrination will be reassigned back to the fleet.

The famous Hotel del Coronado is the backdrop for boat drills. But the close proximity of tourists, who enjoy watching the future SEALs train, doesn't mean there will be any letup in the work. The hotel's elegance and beauty are in stark contrast to the rugged men who are working so hard to look tough to the onlookers. The teams have been training along this beautiful beach since their inception.

When a trainee makes a mistake or can't complete an exercise, he hears about it from an instructor. Usually this in done in a soft voice and a face-to-face confrontation. Instructors don't have to yell to be heard or understood. The class quickly learns that there are no excuses for not completing a particular exercise during morning physical training. The penalty is another trip to the surf and sand, followed by making up for the lost series of exercises. Sometimes the entire class pays for a single man's mistake.

The entire class runs along the beautiful strip of beach at Coronado. Some of the men are very strong runners and pull away from the group, hoping that a first-place finish will earn them a few minutes' rest while the losers earn some time in the surf. Instructors run along the course to make sure none of the trainees have any problems. Most of the instructors are good long-distance runners themselves, making them the ones for the class to beat.

Trainees climb over another obstacle on the obstacle course. After a man has completed the course, he has used every muscle in his body several times. The wide variety of obstacles test speed, strength, and coordination. If mistakes are made, time is taken out to do 20 pushups and is counted in the total run time. So it's important to complete each obstacle correctly.

BUD/S and its predecessors have been training Navy frogmen and SEALs since the early 1950s. At one time BUD/S training also was conducted on the East Coast at the naval amphibious base in Little Creek, Virginia. Now, all basic training, as well as advanced SEAL training, is conducted at Coronado's amphibious base. Coronado is a near-island that sits in the center of San Diego Bay. It is connected at its southernmost tip to the mainland by way of a narrow, eight-mile-long sand spit called the Silver Strand. The Naval Amphibious Base Coronado is located on the northern portion of this narrow strand, just south of the village of Coronado. The north end of Coronado proper is occupied by the massive Naval Air Station North Island. Known as NAS North Island, this facility is a major maintenance, training, and repair depot for the naval air arm of the Pacific fleet. Naval aviators have been flying from North Island since 1911, when flight instructor Glenn Curtiss officially opened the first military aviation school in the United States. The first naval aircraft carrier, the USS *Langley*, moored at North Island in 1924 and pioneered naval aviation in the Pacific. Today, North Island is home for three West Coast–based aircraft carriers. The Naval Amphibious Base Coronado, also built on reclaimed land in 1943, is a relative newcomer.

A roll in the sand is required after every punishment trip to the surf. Any trainee who doesn't come back covered with enough sand gets another trip to the surf, while the rest of the class gets to do pushups. This treatment and punishment is constant throughout training, often resulting in a dozen or so sandy interludes each day. Trainees learn to ignore the dirt, grime, and cold, which is good preparation for combat conditions.

An instructor dumps sand on a trainee who hasn't paid attention to another instructor. While this treatment may seem insensitive or cruel, it's distributed equally to everyone. As everyone soon learns, there are enough instructors to keep track of everything that happens in a class. Every man gets sand shoveled on himself several times during each day's boat drills.

Nestled between North Island's naval air station and the much smaller naval amphibious base on the Silver Strand is the resort community of Coronado. To call Coronado idyllic is an understatement; it is a neat, manicured residential setting of expensive homes with broad, white sand beaches on the Pacific side and the San Diego skyline on the bay side. Anchoring the western end of Orange Avenue, a palm-lined main boulevard of restaurants, boutiques, and art galleries, is the famous Hotel del Coronado. The historic hotel has been a favorite of presidents, royalty, and movie stars for more than a century. When it was built in 1887, it was the largest resort hotel in the world. Thomas Edison personally installed the electric lights during its construction.

Sometimes the only rest a man gets is standing at attention waiting for an instructor to give directions for the next event. Almost always the rest comes while the trainee is wet, cold, and tired. Summer classes have the advantage of a warm sun to dry the trainees out a bit, but unfortunately this also results in getting sunburned.

One of the more interesting, and difficult, training events is drown-proofing. With hands and ankles bound, trainees must jump into the deep end of the combat pool and "survive" for 30 minutes. The first time they must learn how to relax and breathe without the use of normal swim strokes. Of course, the instructors have demonstrated the method and rhythm of breath holding, breath release, bouncing up easily from the bottom, getting new air, and starting the process over again. It requires concentration and patience in the water.

Today, the hotel stands as an elegant, architectural monument to the grace and splendor of a past era. Just south of the Hotel del Coronado, between the hotel and the amphibious base, is a series of modern high-rise beach condominiums. Fewer than 300 yards from the concrete condo towers on this gorgeous strip of golden beach, the United States Navy conducts the toughest military training in the world.

While every time a man practices drown-proofing is a test, this final test lasts for more than an hour. Each man must stay in one place for about 15 minutes, simply breathing, bouncing off the bottom, and repeating the process over again. Then he must swim laps, with hands and legs still bound, and return to the deep end for more bounce breathing. All who are able to complete this test and have not dropped out of training can swim in this manner for hours upon end if necessary. Later, the trainees will learn to escape the bindings underwater.

Once individual men have learned the basic technique of survival in the water with hands and legs bound, larger groups spend more time practicing. A simple dolphin kick by a strong swimmer will easily propel a man to the surface every minute for air. Trainees have already learned to hold their breath comfortably for a minute during underwater knot tying.

SEAL trainees spend a major part of each week in the combat pool. They are taught some of the finer techniques of swim strokes that are used when carrying equipment in the water. Their basic stroke is a sidestroke using their legs and fins. This leaves their arms and hands free for carrying equipment and weapons. These trainees must constantly account for each other's, and their own, safety. Signaling you are safe is done with arm and hand signals and a loud "hoo-yah" shout.

Once in awhile the fastest man in a given event, like underwater knot tying, gets special attention. This trainee was so quick that his instructor decided to have him demonstrate to the entire class. While he didn't set a new record, his time was less than 25 seconds surface to surface. Some of the trainees are natural swimmers, generally called pool rats, and seem to enjoy their time in the water. All of the instructors are pool rats and have no problem holding their breath underwater for more than a minute at a time.

Navy SEALs must know how to tie several knots well, as must all naval personnel. However, SEALS must tie them underwater. They are taught and tested in two-man teams. One trainee watches and waits while his swim buddy ties his knots. On land, this wouldn't be too difficult, but tying five knots each underwater can take up to a minute. If a man makes a mistake, he spends more time underwater, until the instructor gives the signal to surface or one of the trainees is forced, from lack of air, to surface.

A trainee climbs the rope ladder as he practices his skill on the object that is found on most ships, as the means of entry into smaller boats, and into the water for divers and swimmers. Trainees must learn to move efficiently up and down the ladder, as they will be required to do it later in open seas and with other men on the same ladder. As with many of the obstacles in the course, it's easy to complete at a slow pace but requires learning the proper technique for speed. And speed is what the instructors demand.

The images in this book are a silent testimony to the rigorous training that is BUD/S. But if these likenesses were to find their voice, it would be the hoarse, throaty cry of "hoo-yah" shouted by BUD/S trainees. The origin of the term hoo-yah is unclear. It originated on the West Coast, as it was seldom heard on the East Coast during those years when the Navy conducted Basic Underwater Demolition Team/SEAL training on both coasts.

One theory attributes the expression to a popular mid-1950s underwater demolition team instructor named Bud Juric. An aggressive volleyball player, he used to yell "poo-yah" when he spiked the ball. It is said that the trainees of that era took the term and converted it to "hoo-yah." Other old SEALs claim that another BUD/S instructor in the mid-1950s named Paul McNalley coined the term. A third theory holds that earlier training classes simply adopted a syllabic reversal of "yahoo." Whatever the origin, it has evolved into a universal trainee response during all phases of BUD/S training and a favored expression in the teams.

Once the class has walked the obstacle course a few times, trainees will have learned the techniques required to run through each obstacle. The rope bridge is easy to maneuver at a slow pace, but on the run it requires coordination as well as strength. Eventually the class learns that only one man at a time can move across it fast. More than one man on the bridge causes it to jump up and down, taking precious time from the overall run. And they have also learned that slow trips through the course often require a second trip.

Two instructors walk through a group of trainees as the class starts its day with an extensive physical exercise on the sandy beach behind the BUD/S compound at the amphibious base. No matter how many pushups the trainees did the previous day, they seem to do more the next day. Instructors watch each trainee closely to see that each exercise is done properly. Physical training isn't done for punishment, although it may seem that way; it's done to build the proper physical strength for being an active-duty SEAL.

As the class progresses toward the boat-drill training phase, trainees still take several trips through the obstacle course. This course will prepare the men for just about every test the body will experience in swimming, diving, parachuting, hand-to-hand combat, running with equipment, and a host of other requirements a SEAL faces each day. By the time each man has been through the course a dozen times, he begins to learn how to maneuver it with speed and confidence. As always, the fastest get a rest at the end and the slowest get another opportunity to improve their last run.

Standing at attention, cold and covered with sand from a recent trip into the surf, trainees contemplate what happens next. They are tired to the bone, cold, wet, and dirty, and it's still early in the afternoon of a long day of work. The basic principle of BUD/S indoctrination training is simple: Weed out those who can't mentally and physically take the brutal punishment of endless exercise under stressful conditions. Those who mentally accept that the program is simple, but not easy, begin to understand that they can make it.

BUD/S trainees crawl up the beach from a trip into the surf during a break in morning physical training exercises. They must crawl fast enough to make the instructors happy or return to the surf as a class. The cold water takes its toll on many of the men, who seem to welcome the seemingly endless exercises as a way to warm up for a few minutes. Morning physical training exercise programs will be a part of the everyday life of a Navy SEAL but probably will not be as intensive as during BUD/S training.

Each day of Class 228's Indoc seems to be a little longer and a little more intense than the previous one. Each morning of Indoc begins at the pool at 0500 hours. After a two-hour pool evolution that is half physical harassment and half water training, the students don their fatigues and boots. When they are fully dressed, the instructors usually order them back into the pool with their gear. They then run wet and cold to the chow hall for a quick breakfast and back across the base to the special warfare center to continue their training.

Days, and sometimes nights, at BUD/S are a series of training evolutions. As the days become weeks, the evolutions seem endless. The students run a minimum of six miles each day to the chow hall, just to eat. BUD/S trainees live on the run and are always cold and wet. When they are at the special warfare center, they make several trips a day to the Pacific Ocean and are made to roll on the beach after returning from the surf. Now they are cold, wet, and sandy. Yet along with the harassment and misery, there is the teaching. The real

THE TEST

SO YOU WANNA BE A FROGMAN

Want to become a Navy SEAL? Want to take the challenge of Basic Underwater Demolition/SEAL (BUD/S) training? Maybe become part of the best fighting military special forces in the world? Well, as many SEALs would say, the only easy day was yesterday.

The Navy's requirements for admission to Basic Underwater Demolition/SEAL training are straightforward and simple. Applicants must be males under the age of 29 who have passed a written exam not much different than college entry and SAT tests. Navy recruiters will be happy to administer this written examination before you sign up for a hitch.

Obviously, candidates must be in good mental and physical health. They also must be in good physical condition and pass the following test in less than an hour:

1. *Swim 500 yards using breaststrokes or sidestrokes in less than 12.5 minutes.*

2. *Run 1.5 miles in military boots in less than 11.5 minutes.*

3. *Do 42 pushups in two minutes.*

4. *Do 50 sit-ups in two minutes.*

5. *Do six pull-ups.*

Sounds pretty easy, and it should be easy for the average high school senior who has participated in some regular athletic program. Physical conditioning and endurance are much more important than size in potential candidates, as larger men have had more difficulty with some of the training. Bodybuilders are usually the first to drop out.

Men who pass the basic requirements, a medical examination, and the Navy's enlistment requirements can sign up for the Navy and Basic Underwater Demolition/SEAL training and other specialized schools. Because each individual's credentials and education level is different, those enlistment requirements must be learned by talking with a Navy recruiter. The more education you have completed before entering the Navy, the more desirable you will be as a SEAL candidate, and the more options you will have regarding an enlistment or possible career in the Navy.

Men who fail SEAL training—and the vast majority do fail—are still in the Navy and must meet the obligation that they agreed to when joining. That's why you should consider your enlistment options very

A statue of a creature from the swamps greets new trainees to Basic Underwater Demolition/SEAL training. The requirements to graduate from training aren't complicated and barely fill a single-spaced typed page. And while they may be simple, they are not easy.

Running is a large part of Navy SEAL training. Men in the program run everywhere they go: to chow, to the bathroom, to class, and to bed at night. And they also are expected to make at least one long-distance beach run every day, rain or shine. Trainees are pushed by instructors who run every step along with the class.

carefully. Only the serious and well-prepared man should consider this very demanding program.

If you're serious about becoming a Navy SEAL after reading this book and learning the minimum requirements, then starting a one-year program to reach that goal would be a good idea before talking to a Navy recruiter. If you are not a college graduate, it is suggested that you attend a community college and take such courses as physics and advanced mathematics. You also should run and swim several miles each and every day, stopping to do 20 or 30 pushups every few minutes. Although you do not need to be a qualified sport diver, parachutist, or marksman, these accomplishments certainly won't hurt.

But nothing, physically or mentally, will prepare you for the long, cold, and physically exhausting days of SEAL team training. No matter how hard you prepare for this training, your preparation time will be easy compared to the real thing.

Physical fitness is key for success in the SEAL program. Men in the program do several hundred pushups every day, mostly as punishment for being too slow or making a mistake. They spend several hours climbing over difficult obstacles located on a bed of hot sand. They also do a morning physical training program that would cause a wide receiver in the NFL to run short of breath.

Swimming is at the heart of Navy SEAL training. Men in the program spend several hours every day in the pool, bay, and open ocean. They are expected to make long swims in heavy equipment and rough waters. They are expected to hold their breath for a long time underwater. They also are expected to swim with hands and feet bound.

The class returns from a four-mile run on the soft sand tired and dirty. This run is another of the daily events during this early phase of training. Most of the men are conditioned to the runs by the second week, when more strenuous boat drills begin. And by now, the bulk of those who weren't in the peak of physical condition have DORed (dropped on request). The next week of serious boat work will also take its toll on the class.

purpose of Indoc, as the men in Class 228 are constantly reminded, is to prepare them for the physical ordeal that will begin in First Phase. They also begin to learn skills they will need as Navy SEALs.

The instructors appear insensitive and often cruel. A great deal of what they do is to test the spirit and character of their charges, individually and as a class. They are instructors, but they are also gatekeepers, and they take this job very seriously. At times the instructors seem arbitrary and almost sadistic. But then something happens. They become teachers instead of tormentors. An instructor who has just sent the class into the surf or dropped them for pushups will suddenly become quite civil. It's a Jekyll-and-Hyde routine. Most trainees understand this, and there is a truce of sorts. The punishment is put on hold and the BUD/S trainees become students.

The teaching begins in the pool. I noted many changes at BUD/S since I graduated, but the most dramatic are in the swimming curriculum. In the past, it was simply a matter of showing the trainees a basic stroke and making them swim laps—kick, stroke, and glide. Now it's all about technique. The instructors begin with teaching buoyancy control and body position in the water. The basic stroke is a modified side-stroke that the trainees will later adapt to the use of fins. Trainees do lengths in the pool using just their legs. Then they are taught a new method of breathing, rolling in the water to get a breath rather than lifting their heads. It's called "swimming downhill." Here, BUD/S swimmers learn to glide through the water, using their feet and fins as if ascending downhill, rather than fighting and pulling their way along with choppy hand strokes. As the trainees practice, the instructors are right there, coaching and teaching.

During the first week of Indoc, the trainees practice surface-swimming skills without fins. The second week they put on standard-issue duck feet. The instruction and coaching continue, along with the physical harassment. A number of other pool competency skills are taught during Indoc. There are basic knots that the

A wet, dirty, and hot class returns from completing a four-mile run along the Silver Strand Beach. Today, the entire class was slow and had to make several trips into the surf, followed by a roll in the sand. The trainees compete to be the first runner back to base so that they can avoid another trip into the water.

A boat crew drags its boat across the sand, learning to both carry and control their movements as a team. The craft isn't all that heavy at 150 pounds, but it is unwieldy and cumbersome to move fast. Each man must keep his balance in the soft sand, run in step with the others, and not slip. A fall by one man pulls the entire team down. By the end of the afternoon, it will seem like a thousand pounds of boat to the tired crew.

trainees need to know and be able to tie underwater while holding their breath. These are knots they will later use to rig underwater explosives in simulated combat conditions. The Indoc instructors explain each knot, some of its applications, and how it can be tied quickly underwater. Each student carries a section of line, which is tied to the neck of his canteen, to practice with and to take into the water for knot-tying drills.

Along with knot tying, the trainees are graded on underwater swimming. In Indoc, they have to swim underwater without fins for 35 meters. The secret to underwater swimming is going deep early. The trainees learn that if they swim along the bottom in deeper water, the increased partial pressure of oxygen in their lungs will allow them to hold their breath longer and swim farther.

The most intimidating of the pool competency skills is drown-proofing. Trainees' ankles are bound together and their hands are tied behind their back. Trussed in this manner, they are introduced to a number of underwater maneuvers and drills they will be required to perform during First Phase. The point of these exercises is to teach trainees to be comfortable in the water and to stay calm. The instructors constantly remind them to relax, but it's not easy for some. Alert instructors, with fins and masks, swim among them like sharks, looking for a trainee who may be on the verge of drowning.

Next to swimming, the obstacle course is the most technically demanding challenge for the Indoc trainees. Trainees have to negotiate 15 major obstacles, including a series of walls, vaults, rope bridges, and logs, with a short sprint in the soft sand between obstacles. On the first day at the "O-course," the instructors walk the trainees through the course and explain the various ways to handle each barrier. Then each member of the class runs it for time. This is not a confidence course, as some are called. These are real obstacles, and the Indoc trainees struggle with their first attempt.

Two boat crews pass each other as they prepare for surf passage. The crews must learn to work together as they maneuver the craft both in and out of the water. At first the task is difficult. But after several drills and several trips into the surf, the crews begin to learn to handle the boats well.

The senior SEAL class instructor, called a proctor, walks the beach during one of the many open-water boat drills. It's his job to see that the class moves efficiently and safely through each of the day's well-planned events. It's also his job to keep a written account of each student's training times and progress.

Boat crews must take their small, 13-foot craft into the Pacific Ocean surf off Coronado and return to the shore quickly. The first few times are an exciting thing for many of the crews, who quickly learn the craft will easily capsize when hit by a large wave. The crew must right the boat and row quickly for the beach because the last team will have to pay a penalty for its mistakes.

This boat crew returns from their "congratulations run" into the surf after completing the week of difficult drills. The group moves the boat with speed and coordination, looking like a well-trained unit, which it has become. Somehow, the water doesn't seem as cold and the sand not as dirty now that they have made it into the next phase of training. They have learned what it means to be a team and will operate as a team throughout their SEAL training.

Indoctrination also introduces Class 228 to group physical training. Physical training includes a full range of highly regimented calisthenics led by an instructor. First Phase trainees do physical training on the famous BUD/S grinder, the blacktop expanse in the middle of the main BUD/S compound. Indoc trainees do not have that privilege; they must do their training on the beach behind the BUD/S compound.

No single exercise, in itself, is too strenuous or difficult, and many are designed to balance and stretch certain muscle groups. But two muscle areas are hammered again and again: abs and arms. Each third or fifth exercise is a set of pushups, usually a

count of 20 but often as many as 50. For the abdomen, there are sit-ups and leg levers, but the exercise of choice at BUD/S is flutter kicks.

Again and again, the trainees will be on their backs, legs six inches off the deck. In this position they will count off flutter kicks with their legs straight and toes pointed. This exercise builds stomach muscles and will help prepare the trainees for long ocean swims later in training. While one instructor calls the cadence and leads the class in exercises, the other instructors walk among the trainees offering encouragement and a liberal dose of verbal harassment. During physical training, the class must show spirit

Boat crews stand silently at attention, waiting for instructors to inspect their craft. By now they have learned the many rules and procedures required during these and other indoctrination exercises. Every boat crew looks as though it has done this a hundred times, which the crews probably have in the past few days. The boats are clean and every item is in its proper place. For once during this long set of drills, no crew has to hit the surf as punishment. The class proctor says, "Congratulations. You've made it through indoctrination. Hit the surf."

and motivation and loudly maintain the exercise count. If it doesn't, the instructor leading training will periodically send trainees into the cold surf with the following command: "Get wet and sandy."

BUD/S trainees live on the run. The uniform for physical training and the beach runs is a white T-shirt, long pants, and boots. Several times during the runs the men of Class 228 are sent up and over the large berm dunes, across the hard sand, and into the surf. Cold, wet, and sandy is a permanent condition for a BUD/S class, and the condition will take its toll. As in all BUD/S classes, even in Indoc, some in Class 228

decide that the price for becoming a Navy SEAL is too steep. They decide to drop out of training.

During the second week of Indoc, Class 228 begins IBS surf passage. IBS officially means inflatable boat, small. Unofficially, it's the "itty bitty ship." Up to this point, trainees have functioned as individuals and as a class. Now they will learn to perform as boat crews. A crew is made up of six to eight men. In the SEAL teams, the basic combat unit is the same size, only it will be called a squad or fire team. During all training, especially Hell Week, boat crews have to function as a team.

Boat crews that dump their craft in the heavy surf or return to the beach last cause the entire class to hold in the pushup position for several minutes. After that, the boat crew that finished last must head back into the surf for another try, while the other crews clean their craft and get a brief rest.

The IBS is an unwieldy, 150-pound, 13-foot rubber boat. It would be a miserable choice as a recreational boat for navigating a white-water river. They are poorly designed and too cumbersome for just about anything except teaching BUD/S trainees to work together in the surf zone, to pull together as a team. Initially, Class 228 learns the procedures and protocol for rigging the small boats and aligning them on the beach for inspection. When the boats are rigged and the trainees are ready, the men, in lifejackets, stand at attention by their boats. Their fatigue hats are attached to their shirts by a length of orange parachute cord. The paddles are wedged in a particular manner between the main tube and the two cross tubes of the boat. Bow and stern lines are carefully coiled on the rubber floor.

After each surf-passage race, the crews must return to this same spot, prepare their craft for inspection, and wait at attention for the next race.

In front of the line of boats, the coxswains, or boat crew leaders, stand in a line abreast holding their paddles at the order-arms position, as if the paddles were some kind of long-barreled rifles. In turn, each coxswain salutes the instructor in charge and reports his boat rigged and his crew ready for sea. Meanwhile, the other instructors roam the line of boats looking for discrepancies. If they find a paddle that is not tightly stowed, they fling it across the beach. If a student runs to retrieve it without his swim buddy, the whole boat crew drops for pushups. During IBS drills, trainees do pushups with their boots atop the main

As this introduction portion of training nears an end, the men left standing are proud of making it through one of the most difficult physical training programs in the entire military. They pose for a quick photo before the next phase of their training begins.

tube of their boat and their hands down on the sand. The coxswains brief their men and then direct them as they paddle out through the surf zone, clear of the breakers, and back. These surf drills are contests. There are winners and losers. A winning crew may get to sit out a race. For the losers, it's more surf, cold water, and sand.

The last day of Indoc for Class 228 is graduation day for Class 225. Like the seasons, BUD/S is an endless cycle. Classes come and go. Inevitably, they become smaller in the process. Class 228 attends in a tight formation, dressed in starched fatigues, spit-shined boots, and starched covers. There are now 68 men left. As they prepare for the serious business of First Phase training, they watch with understandable envy as Class 225 heads off for advanced SEAL training. This is all part of the ritual—part of the change of seasons.

Class 228 learns what's required of it, as a previous class demonstrates a quick morning physical training session on the compound grinder. The earlier class has trained together and learned what the instructors expect in the way of timing and performance. Rarely is a man out of step with his teammates. Still, the men are sent into the surf twice during the brief period. Their last exercise is to order the new class, which just started its second phase of training, into the surf.

CONDITIONING

The trainees start the first phase of Basic Underwater Demolition/SEAL (BUD/S) training with a brisk four-mile run down the long beach. This is a warmup for the many days of physical conditioning ahead. Trainees learned a great deal about conditioning during indoctrination, and all of them are now in excellent shape. However, it isn't enough. Now they will learn what it physically takes to be a Navy SEAL. They will repeat everything they did during indoctrination, using their times and numbers from that period as a base from which to improve. That indoctrination will seem easy by the time they reach Second Phase.

It's Monday, October 18, the first day of First Phase training. The class is arrayed in boots, long fatigue pants, and white T-shirts. This is its first physical training inside the Basic Underwater Demolition/SEAL (BUD/S) training compound, an honor reserved for First Phase trainees. They stand in places marked by miniature frog flippers painted on the blacktop. The paint and macadam are chipped and stained where generations of BUD/S trainees have toiled and suffered. They are armed only with canteens, which stand in formation alongside each trainee.

There is a raised platform on the north side of the BUD/S grinder. The three-foot-high platform bears tall

gold letters of the senior BUD/S class, Class 226, now in Third Phase. From here, an instructor leads Class 228 in its initial First Phase physical training session. The rest of the instructors move among the class like prowling lions, tearing into individual trainees. Two of them roam among the lines of struggling trainees with water hoses, blasting their shaved heads with a stream of cold water. Sixty-eight men remain in First Phase conditioning for Class 228, down 30 from the class of 98 men who started training a week earlier. By a conservative count, this group will do more than 500 pushups and 60 pull-ups before First Phase training is an hour old. The instructor leading physical training

An instructor pours water on the senior class petty officer, which may be a welcome cooling, as the man accounts for the entire class. The senior officers and petty officers must know where every man is at all times. In turn, each man must know where his teammate is at all times. Not knowing not only will cause the entire class to make several punishment trips into the surf, but it may bring the erring teammates a safety violation. Such violations are important and serious lessons. Too many, and a man may face being dropped from training.

The class now performs its morning physical training exercises in perfect sync. The class has learned that this is more difficult to accomplish than the exercises themselves. And it never gets easier, as the instructor holds the class in a bent position for several minutes. When someone wavers or falls, the entire class must hit the surf and get sandy. No matter how well the class performs, one of the instructors will see a mistake or help trainees create one.

First Phase instructors are among the best SEALs on active duty. Each of the instructors can easily do everything that is physically expected of the BUD/S class. In fact, they relish being the one who makes a beach run the fastest or leads exercises at the head of a class. They seem to never break a sweat or get tired. That's because, as the class will eventually learn, this phase of training is easy compared to what the instructors have gone through to become SEALs and BUD/S instructors.

takes them from one exercise to the next with no break. For good measure, he mixes in an extra ration of flutter kicks and sit-ups.

Class 228 knew this was coming. Tales of the trauma of the first day of First Phase were passed on to them by 226 and 227, but neither Indoc nor warnings from the senior classes prepared them for the intensity of this physical training session. For the First Phase instructors, it is a calculated mayhem, designed to force each man in the class to reassess his personal commitment to the goal of becoming a Navy SEAL. Many in Class 228 are saying to themselves, "Four weeks of this, then Hell Week. I don't know if I can do it!" But they will have to if they want to become Navy SEALs.

Lashed to a stanchion just outside the First Phase office is the famous BUD/S bell. Tradition calls for a student who quits in First Phase to ring the bell three times and place his helmet on the grinder. Indoc drop on requests don't count. The helmets that marked the attrition of Class 227 are gone. It's a change of season, and the bell first tolls for Class 228 that morning. One of the class members has found this training not to his liking. He rings the bell three times and places his helmet on the grinder. He gets a warm shower, a clean set of clothing, and a hot meal.

Many think the bell is a tradition that dates back to the early days of Navy frogmen training. Not so. When the current BUD/S training compound was built

When a man DORs (drops training on request), tradition requires him to ring the bell three times and place his helmet on the grinder. Midway through First Phase, the line of helmets has grown and the bell has sounded many times. Every SEAL, instructor, and trainee stops what he is doing when the bell rings. That's because each one of them knows how hard the training is and the toll it takes. And each one of them knows that no matter how difficult the training is, it's even harder to ring the bell.

The entire class takes its first important timed run. Trainees will have 32 minutes to make the four miles in the round trip, all of it in the mixed soft and hard sands of a high tide. It's also a very warm day in the San Diego area. By now most of the men should be able to run several eight-minute miles in a row, but the previous week's physical exercise has drained them in the endurance department. The line of men strings out a few hundred yards, but most of the runners stick with a good pace.

The wheel of misfortune, usually called the wheel of pain by trainees, stands as a quiet reminder of what the punishment can be if a serious mistake is made. At this point in their physical training, there is little room for any mistakes. But, of course, the instructors can easily find mistakes or create something that will cause a mistake. When something is a serious error, or nears a safety violation, the man gets to spin the wheel.

Those not making the run under the prescribed time of 32 minutes pay a heavy price. They spend the better part of an hour doing the same exercises completed in the morning. Only this time, they get to do them in the soft sand and wet surf. The only break is a trip into the surf and a roll in the hot sand. A dozen trainees have to do the punishment exercises.

in 1970, training moved from the World War II–vintage Quonset huts on the amphibious base to the new facility on the Pacific side of the Silver Strand Highway. Before 1970, trainees who wanted to drop on request went to the instructor's hut, banged three times on the door jamb with their helmets, and yelled, "I quit." Master Chief Terry Moy was a legendary instructor at BUD/S in the late 1960s and early 1970s. "Mother Moy," as he was called, moved across the Silver Strand Highway with BUD/S when the SEALS occupied the new facility. Moy, Class 35, was an old-school frogman who was justly proud of his new office quarters. When the first trainee banged on his new door to quit, he had to put a stop to it—not the quitting

but the abuse of his new door. The next day he brought in a tugboat bell and lashed it to the stanchion outside the First Phase office. Except for the three-year exile in the early 1990s, when the bell was removed because it was thought to be demeaning, Mother Moy's bell has been there ever since.

After the brutal first-day physical training session on the grinder and a four-mile run for breakfast, Class 228 faces its first timed evolution in First Phase. It's a terrible day for running on the beach. The tide is dead high, which means the class will have to thread its way along the high watermark between the soft dry sand and the not-so-soft wet sand. The cutoff for this first timed run is 32 minutes. Eight-minute miles don't

Pushing and pulling old and rough logs often causes blisters and cut hands when a slip is made. This happens on a regular basis because the men are tired. Medical corpsmen stand by to repair the frequent injuries, which usually have been cleaned by a trip into the surf. After a few days, hands become accustomed to the logs and are tough enough to withstand the rare slip of a team.

This trainee moves along a log during the first phase of training. In this phase of training, trainees become well acquainted with logs. There are dozens of logs to jump over and crawl under at the obstacle course. Even more logs have to be hoisted up onto their shoulders. These pushup logs are 160 pounds, and the men must carry them through various exercises as a team.

Upper body strength is required as this trainee pushes himself over one of the obstacle course logs. The hundreds of daily pushups have prepared him for this difficult part of the course. Those who slip get to try again after dropping for 20 pushups.

The final days of boat drills are here, and the crews are experienced and ready. Now they are told to intentionally dump their boats in the surf and right them again. All the crews have been doing this by accident, so they accomplish the task with no problems. Still, the fastest crews get a rest and the slowest crews get another trip into the surf. Most know that this is their last time with the boats for a few days.

sound too demanding, but at high tide and in wet trousers and boots, it's not an easy run. Those who make the run in the allotted time are given time to slowly jog in the soft sand to cool down. Those who don't make their time do flutter kicks in the surf and endure the 60-degree water. Then they move on to the next evolution: log physical training.

Log physical training is older than the Navy frogmen of World War II. A colorful officer by the name of Draper Kauffman is considered the father of underwater demolition teams. After the staggering losses suffered by the Marines at Tarawa in World War II, Kauffman

was sent to Fort Pierce, Florida, to train men who would go onto the landing beaches ahead of the Marines. Prior to his service in the U.S. Navy and our entry into World War II, Kauffman served as an ambulance driver and bomb disposal expert in England. There he observed the newly formed British commandos exercising with sections of telephone poles to build strength and teamwork. He introduced those same techniques at Fort Pierce when he began to train the first Navy frogmen. Much like surf drills with the inflatable boats, log physical training encourages teamwork and spirit. It also pays to be a winner.

Trainees lie with their finned feet fluttering in the air. Later they will do this exercise while they place their heads in the water. This isn't a punishment; rather, it is an exercise to familiarize them with having a mask full of water and heavy fins. The exercise also builds strong stomach and leg muscles, much the same as drown-proofing. While the class did this during the earlier phase, now it becomes more important as the diving phase moves a little closer.

The beach runs never seem to stop or be the same as the previous one. And the instructors always know exactly how long the average runner needs to complete the chosen course. Midway through Phase One, the final timed run takes place. For once all of the runners are closely bunched and make the prescribed time. There will be no punishment singled out; however, the entire class still gets to hit the surf and cool off.

The trainees jump into the pool as they are about to complete one of the most critical tests during this phase—the 50-meter underwater pool swim. Most of the men are comfortable in the pool and can make the swim with ease. Two or three need to be pulled out and receive instructions before making their second attempts. A medical corpsman keeps close watch to ensure that there are no mishaps.

BUD/S trainees must do two-mile open-ocean swims. They must enter the ocean through the surf, giving their name to an instructor on a boat 100 yards out to sea. Then, with his swim mate, each trainee swims a mile down to the Hotel del Coronado rocks and back. Each team is timed and must make the circuit in less than 95 minutes. The entire class makes it in well under this time and earns a run over the sand berm for a hot shower.

This trainee takes a few moments to rest at the half-way point in his open-water swim. Even though the San Diego Bay water is cold, at about 60 degrees, the swimmers are warm in wet suits and hoods. This is a pass or fail open-water swim test and all of the class succeeds.

When the instructors arrive at the log physical training area, Class 228 is standing by its logs, one log for each boat crew of six to eight men. The trainees now wear their long-sleeved fatigue shirts buttoned to the collar and soft hats. Each log is eight feet long and one foot in diameter. They weigh about 160 pounds.

Between the log physical training area, which is directly behind the BUD/S training compound, and the Pacific is a 15-foot-high, dune-like sand berm built by the Seabees to protect the compound from the winter storm surf. Class 228 charges up the berm and down to the surf some 50 yards away. Once again the trainees are cold and wet. On the way back they roll down the berm to the log physical training area. The boat crews retrieve their logs and head back for the surf. Finally, the trainees circle up and learn the basic exercises for log physical training: squats, jumping jacks, sit-ups, and overhead tosses. Most of these are four-count exercises. Log physical training puts a premium on teamwork and spirit. Strength is important, but secondary.

The boat crews gradually begin to get the hang of working together. They talk it up, motivate each other, and pull as a team. As with most BUD/S evolutions, there are winners and losers. The boat crews compete in various races using their logs in a similar fashion to the way they used their small inflatable boats in training. For the winners, there are a few minutes of rest. For the losers, there's additional log training. After log training, Class 228 trades its logs for the small inflatable boats (IBSs) and hits the surf.

Tuesday, day two of First Phase, is not an easy day, but it is nothing like the trauma of Monday. Next to Hell Week, the first week of First Phase causes the greatest percentage of attrition. It's as if some of the trainees simply wanted to get to First Phase before they dropped out. Somehow, there is less shame in quitting during BUD/S phase training than during Indoc. Much of the first week's attrition comes on the first day, but it goes on all week. The evolutions take their toll on the class. The most demanding are the conditioning runs, log

At this stage in training, trainees have only faced rough surf in their small boats. Now they must undertake rock portage in that same surf. It's one of the most dangerous exercises they will attempt and requires teamwork. They must paddle into the rocks, riding with the surf, and drag their boat on shore. Then they have to return to the water again. They must do this at least three times.

physical training, and IBS surf-passage races. All are conducted with liberal doses of harassment from the First Phase staff. In all evolutions, the winners get a brief break from training and the losers earn more torment. From the trainee's perspective, the punishment handed out by the instructors seems capricious and arbitrary. In fact, these are very well-planned and closely monitored evolutions, calculated to test the desire and spirit of those who want to be SEALs.

During the first week of First Phase, Class 228 prepares for open-water swimming. For the first time, trainees don fins in the pool and begin doing laps using the accepted modified sidestroke. In the teams, they'll swim with any fins they like, but at BUD/S they wear the same standard duck feet that have been used by frogmen since the 1950s. After instruction, critique, and lap swimming, it's harassment time. The

trainees are made to lie on their backs with their heads over the edge of the pool. With their masks full of water and heads tilted back, they do flutter kicks. The class did this during Indoc, but now with the addition of the big duck feet, the flutter kicks are much harder. With stomach muscles burning, they have to sing the BUD/S version of "Take Me Out to the Ball Game":

Take me out to the surf zone,
Take me out to the sea,
Make me do pushups and jumping jacks,
I don't care if I never get back,
For it's root, root, root for the SEAL teams,
If we don't pass, it's a shame,
For it's one, two, three rings you're out
Of the old BUD/S game.

After a full day of rock portage, with little rest, the boat crews attempt the same portage at night. Instructors line the rocks and watch closely as this dangerous exercise is completed. Hand signals are used so that there is no misunderstanding about directions. All of the crews manage through the slippery rocks and crashing surf, dragging their boats up into the night air.

Because the training is relentless and very physical, medical corpsmen SEALs are in constant attendance at all events. Along with the instructors, they keep a watchful eye out for limping, cuts, and bruises. Medical attention is immediate, on the beach or at the sick bay inside the training compound. While some injuries may cause a man to be held out for the next class, most are minor and heal quickly.

Yet there is good reason for the harassment and a purpose to their singing with a face mask full of water. It will help them in Second Phase when they have to breathe underwater from their scuba rigs without a face mask. After a choking, Donald Duck–like version of "The Star Spangled Banner," they're ready for the open water—almost. The first open-water swim is a one-mile bay swim to gauge the relative speed of individuals in the class. This is the one and only time

they swim without a buddy. Swim pairs will be assigned by comparable ability, so a fast man will not have to wait for a slow one on a timed swim.

As with most evolutions, there are inspections and protocol. The instructors inspect the trainees' life jackets and diving knives closely. Both are relics from the past. The inflatable rubber life jackets worn on the chest are identical to the one I trained with in the late 1960s, as is the leather-handled Ka-Bar knife. The

A medical corpsman SEAL examines a trainee who has dropped in the sand during a long run. In this case, as with most runs, the man has simply pushed himself too hard and run out of air. The corpsman will make a judgment as to whether the man has a problem and needs a little rest or has taken the opportunity to get out of finishing the run. Every man must complete every run, swim, and boat drill in the evolution. Running out of breath may bring a short break, but it won't eliminate the event.

temperature in San Diego Bay is a comfortable 66 degrees, so they swim without thermal protection. This is their first and only bay swim on the surface. It is also their shortest. All other swims will be in the open ocean and longer than a mile, but they will be allowed wet-suit tops in the Pacific Ocean.

Perhaps the most critical evolution of the first week, aside from pure survival, is the 50-meter underwater swim. It's 55 yards without fins. Trainees have to do this to continue in First Phase. It's an honest 50 meters—no diving start. The trainees must jump in the water, do a front somersault underwater, and begin their swim across the 25-meter pool. After touching the wall, they swim back. Four trainees are tested at a time. As they turn and head for home, four instructors close in on them, swimming just above and behind. The instructors watch them closely. As they touch the wall, the trailing instructor grabs them by the waistband of their trunks and helps them from the water. A corpsman is there to check each man. Most make it to the finish, but not all.

During week three, they begin rock portage. Rock portage is IBS surf passage with an attitude. The boat crews bust through the breakers in front of the BUD/S compound and head north, just beyond the surf zone. Instead of taking their boats back in across

Early in the day this trainee holds in the upper position of a one-armed pushup. While one-armed pushups aren't usually required in the normal course of training, they become forms of punishment for those not listening to instructors.

the beach, they wait just off the rock jetty in front of the Hotel del Coronado. While curious hotel guests gather to watch, BUD/S instructors signal the boats to come ashore over the rocks. The pile of rocks in front of the hotel are boulders the size of Volkswagens. The boat crews must paddle into the rocks and wrestle their crafts through the surf and over the rocks. It is dangerous business and requires teamwork and courage. For rock portage, a medical officer is always standing by. The crews succeed or fail depending on how well they work together. Getting back into the surf from the rocks is almost as dangerous as coming

ashore. Each boat crew must make three successful landings, then drag its boat back out over the rocks and launch it into the plunging surf. That evening, after dark, Class 228 again paddles its boats north toward the Hotel del Coronado. This time trainees will do rock portage at night. BUD/S trainees will remember night rock portage like naval aviators remember night carrier landings, with respect and a full measure of terror.

Week four, the week before Hell Week, brings more of the same. There are conditioning runs and physical training, surf passage and ocean swims, but

An instructor closely watches as trainees, who were slow to finish the morning run, do pushups in the surf. As part of the punishment for being slow, they have been sent into the cold surf. The training day is less than an hour old and these men are already tired and cold.

each evolution seems to be conducted under a cloud of what is to come the following week.

The instructors keep the pressure on, but they are attentive to trainees who may be limping or have other injuries. The First Phase corpsmen make a point of being a little more approachable. At the same time, the instructors are more intolerant of trainees whose negative attitude or lack of motivation seems to be hurting their boat crews. Officers who show poor

leadership on an evolution are shown no mercy. The First Phase staff is subtly taking ownership of the class. The performance of Class 228 is a reflection of the staff's ability to instruct and motivate.

During week four, the trainees have their last two-mile ocean swim. To be allowed to continue on to Hell Week, they have to make the swim in less than 95 minutes. The ocean temperature is now 59 degrees. The trainees wear wet-suit tops, underwater diving

The entire class, arm in arm, stands in the breaking surf following the hand directions of an instructor. The trainees will sit, move left, move right, and dunk themselves in the cold water. They must work as a team to keep the line from breaking. If the line breaks—and it usually does at first—the class must repeat the exercise until the line holds. The ocean water is cold, and the men must concentrate to keep the line tight.

team life jackets, masks, and fins. First, they swim out through the surf zone to a safety boat waiting 100 yards offshore, just beyond the breakers. They then swim north past the rocks off the Hotel del Coronado and back—one mile up and one back. After checking in with the timekeeper in the boat, they return through the surf to the instructor on the beach. He checks off the swim pairs to fully account for all the trainees who entered the water. Then he drops them for pushups. Two by two, they run up over the berm back to the BUD/S compound. As a class they are strong in the water. All are under the pre–Hell Week 95–minute minimum, and all but three pairs are under the post–Hell Week 85–minute time. This is a tribute to the Indoc instructors who worked with them on swimming technique.

The trainees complete one of the final physical training sessions for Phase One. The training is probably the most physically demanding period of exercise any man will ever complete. Those who have stayed the course are physically tough and ready for anything the BUD/S instructors can throw at them in the next week of training. That's good; they'll need everything they have—because the infamous Hell Week is about to begin.

Week five for Class 228 is very special. It is Hell Week. Hell Week is a familiar and well-choreographed event, but safety considerations and operational details have to be reviewed and individual duties assigned. There are some 64 separate evolutions in Hell Week. Each evolution has a detailed lesson plan, and each has specific written instructions for safety, risk assessment, and supervisory criteria.

This week will test the men in Class 228 to their very core. Each evolution is designed to contribute to the overall goals of Class 228's Hell Week. Those official goals are the following:

Students will demonstrate the qualities
and personal characteristics
of determination, courage, self-sacrifice,
teamwork, leadership, and
a never-quit attitude
under adverse environmental conditions,
fatigue, and stress
throughout Hell Week.

CHAPTER 3
HELL WEEK

BUD/S trainees pile into a mud pyramid during one of the many Hell Week rituals. Every West Coast—trained Navy SEAL has been in the mud flats of San Diego Bay. While all the men are weary from lack of sleep and constant physical activity, they aren't too tired for a chance to mug the camera. It's the one time during their training that dropping for a few pushups isn't going to be given as punishment; the entire week is a never-ending series of punishments.

During Hell Week, running through the soft sand toward the compound at sunset doesn't mean a night's rest is just ahead. It means another sleepless night of cold water, physical exhaustion, and exercise. Most of the men are hoping the class leader is awake enough to keep them headed in the right direction. This is the time most of the trainees wonder if they have made the right choice in volunteering for SEAL training. Several will drop out before the sun rises again.

On most Sunday evenings, the special warfare center is bathed in a soft yellow halogen glow. Invariably there is some activity behind the Basic Underwater Demolition/SEAL (BUD/S) compound and around the student barracks as trainees prepare for the next day's training. Not tonight, not this evening of November 14. The area is completely dark and no one is about—no roving patrols, no student movement, and no one from the watch section checking the back gates. There is a fluorescent bloom from the quarterdeck where two Indoc students sit confined to the reception desk. They have been told to remain at their post and to stay away from the glass doors that lead out to the grinder. Next to the barracks, six small inflatable boats (IBSs) have been readied for rock portage. Helmets with attached chemlites sit perched on the main tube at each paddler's position. Between the chain-link compound fence and the tall beach berm, two large tents wait silently. These will serve as makeshift barracks for the trainees for the next week, where they will be allowed their meager ration of sleep. Inasmuch as Class 228 will have a home during Hell Week, it will be these two canvas shelters.

A file of men in dark clothes and bloused boots emerges from the administration complex on the south side of the grinder. The sliver of moon has not yet risen, and only a few of the brighter stars have found their way through the light sea mist. It is a clammy 60

degrees, about the same temperature as the ocean. The men all wear ball caps, and three of them carry automatic weapons. They move soundlessly across the grinder like a swat team moving into position. As they approach the First Phase classroom, light filtering around the shade on the classroom door reveals that the armed men have ammunition belts clipped around their torsos. The leader gives a signal, and three of the men break away to make their way down the outside hallway to the side door of the classroom. Other dark forms move into position around the grinder. Inside, the 42 men of Class 228 await their fate. They all know it's coming, but not exactly when and how.

It happens quickly. There is a crash as the side door of the classroom is kicked open, the rear door a second later. First there are the whistles—shrill, police-type whistles. Class 228 has been told what to do then it hears a whistle. Trainees hit the deck, cross their legs, and cover their ears with the palms of their hands. The six instructors move in, three from each open door, and the shooting starts.

Mk-43s, the SEAL version of the M-60 machine gun, begin to bark. Although the 7.62mm blank rounds don't have the brisance of live rounds, the noise still is deafening. More whistles, more shouting, and more shooting ensue. And for 60 seconds, nothing can be heard but the sound of gunfire and shouting. The room is lit by muzzle flashes. The machine gunners step over

SEAL instructors move two by two through the trainees, shooting blank rounds and shouting instructions. Trainees are required to hit the ground with hands behind their heads, like prisoners. The attack is meant to keep the men off balance and create confusion about what's happening and what's about to happen. When there is complete silence, the class is ordered into the surf at double time. This week is going to be cold and wet.

and around the prone trainees as they do their work, mindful of the stream of expended shell casings from their weapons. The casings are hot and can cause angry welts if they land on exposed skin. Soon the room is heavy with smoke and the stench of cordite.

"Everybody outside!" an instructor orders.

The 42 members of Class 228 scramble from their previously warm, secure environment that has suddenly turned violent and break out onto the grinder. More whistles blow and they fall to the black-top, covering their ears, with heads down. There they are met with fire hoses, more instructors, and more shooting. Barrels, secure receptacles for the artillery simulators, have been placed around the grinder. Soon there is the scream and boom of imitation artillery rounds to accompany the shooting. Shouting instructors are everywhere, herding trainees to the center of the grinder. The class bunches together on the blacktop as it is assaulted by the fire hoses. Then the whistle drills begin.

Nothing is easy during Hell Week. Boat crews must maneuver their bulky and heavy boats through the obstacle course, against a stopwatch and the other crews. Some of the crews are a man short because so many have dropped out. No exceptions are made for the smaller crews, as there would be no exceptions made if they were operating in a real combat situation. The last-place boat crew will have to hit the surf—with its boat. The others will get a few minutes of rest.

Looking like a group of well-armed commandos, BUD/S instructors attack the training compound, announcing the start of Hell Week. Machine guns rake the walls with blank ammunition, lighting the trainees with muzzle flashes. Dummy explosives erupt and turn the area into the kind of confusion found only in armed conflicts. A whistle pierces the air, and trainees are ordered out into the nightmare week that they will remember for the rest of their lives. Only 40 men remain in the class.

"Fweet!"

The mass of confused students melts to the surface of the grinder. The trainees scoot about on the wet blacktop so their heads are in the direction of the instructor with the whistle.

"Fweet! Fweet!" They begin to crawl toward the sound.

"Fweet! Fweet! Fweet!" They scramble to their feet.

"Fweet!" Back on the grinder—legs crossed, hands over their ears.

For the next hour, they crawl about the grinder, treated to sporadic bursts of machine-gun fire and explosions. Knees and elbows start to abrade on the wet blacktop. The breakout evolution is designed to create chaos and confusion. It sets the tone for this difficult and challenging ordeal. The First Phase staff only can vary the standard fare of noise, shock, and chaos so much. The last Hell Week class was ordered into the grinder before the shooting started. This time the machine gunners assaulted the class inside the classroom.

The class is ordered into the surf, then lined up for a head count. Soon the men are in the soft sand for more whistle drills and more crawling. Then it's

Making a night rock portage in the small inflatable boats was difficult when the class was getting a regular night's sleep. During Hell Week it's a test to keep from drifting off to sleep as each crew's boat rolls along the surf and into the rocks. The men know if they make the portage correctly, an hour or two of sleep awaits them. The possibility of rest and a competition to be the best crew drive everyone through the rocks safely.

back in the water for surf conditioning, better known as surf torture. First, the class spends 15 minutes immersed in a line, arms linked. This is the maximum time allowable at this temperature. For close to an hour, the trainees do a run-paddle-run exercise. The boat crews are sent out through the surf line where they dump the boat, paddle up the beach a few hundred yards, come back in, and then race down the beach with their boat to the starting line. They then trade their boats for logs and begin log physical training in the cold surf. Then it's off to the obstacle course with the boats. The class becomes smaller. Forty-two men have now become 35. They run the O-course in boat crews, hauling the bulky rubber craft over the obstacles.

Another man rings the bell, and the class becomes smaller.

Well after midnight, they paddle north to Hotel del Coronado. This is the first real break for the Hell Week class. They are still cold and wet, but once

beyond the surf line, there are no instructors yelling at them. The serenity of the night on the water seems surreal. They're like shell-shocked infantry troops between artillery barrages. As each boat reaches the Hotel del Coronado, it turns right, paddles shoreward, and crashes into the rocks. For two hours, Class 228 attacks the rocks in front of the Hotel del Coronado in its boats. And a few more trainees ring out.

At 0450 hours, the class brings its boats up to a head carry and begins the shuffle run across the base for breakfast. Before the men eat at the chow hall, they do drills with the small inflatable boats, mostly overhead IBS pushups. When they finally bring the boats down to the ground, the trainees do regular pushups with their feet up on the boats. Once inside the chow hall, the class gets its first rest since breakout the evening before. Well ahead of the rest of the sailors on base, they crowd through the chow line. Two men guard the boats while the rest eat. There are now 32 men. Ten have left in a little under nine hours.

Back at the BUD/S compound, the class pauses briefly at the BUD/S medical clinic for a quick inspection by the medical staff, then heads for the beach. These medical exams will become more comprehensive as the class gets further into Hell Week. The first evolution Monday morning is a two-mile swim. Sixteen pairs of swimmers line up. The instructors work the line of swimmers checking life vests, even though they will not need them; the wet-suit tops will keep them buoyant. The class lumbers into the surf and trainees groan as they trade the sweat inside their wet suits for cold sea water. Two more trainees decide that this is not for them. They walk back ashore and quit. Heads hung and escorted by an instructor, the two trainees walk back to the compound, where they ring the bell. The Hell Week class, still out in the water, is so tired that the bell sounds more like Sunday church bells calling the faithful to worship. After the swim, more beach games and more log physical training follow.

Hell Week is one familiar evolution after another—surf passage, rock portage, log physical training, the obstacle course, runs, swims, long IBS paddles, endless pushups. The men are always cold, wet, and sandy. And the water is cold, just under 60 degrees in the ocean, and colder in San Diego Bay. Everywhere they go—on runs, on the obstacle course, even to chow—they carry the boats on their heads.

Trainees make a run along the high-water line, sloshing water into their boots as the surf rises and falls. Slow runners must drop and do 20 pushups in the cold water. Fast runners do the same thing waiting for others to catch up. Few moments of rest are provided during Hell Week. Otherwise the men would immediately drop off to sleep. Instructors keep a watchful eye to see this doesn't happen too often.

In an afternoon boat drill, crews move with the precision of procedures learned in the previous training phase. The crews look good to instructors, despite being bone tired, and get a short rest as a reward. One of the main objectives of Hell Week is to see if trainees will follow previous procedures unconsciously. Being exhausted and still being able to perform well is a very good test of each man's endurance and his knowledge of each drill.

Boat crews head back to the obstacle course for another round of moving their boats through the barriers. While the teams aren't expected to break any time records, the men move fast. They will hit their second wind several times during the week. They also will walk around like zombies asleep on their feet. Instructors and medical corpsmen keep a tight rein on the class, looking for any potential problems.

Boat crews load up and paddle toward the Hotel del Coronado beach for another rock portage. Having the late afternoon sun on their faces warms the already sleepy crews, who take turns paddling and sleeping. It takes a few more minutes than the last run, but instructors turn a blind eye for the moment. The men will need all their strength and wits to make another portage through the dangerous surf and unforgiving rocks.

Meals are a brief oasis in the middle of the suffering. Before and after entering the mess hall, the instructors put them through physical training and boat drills. Once inside the chow hall, they are given time to eat. After the evening meal, the trainees are put in San Diego Bay for extended immersion drills—and more men quit. With Hell Week just a little more than 24 hours old, the class has been cut in half, and 21 men remain in Class 228.

Monday night begins with a boat-crew olympics of sorts, referred to as Lyon's Lope. Named for the late Scott Lyon, a Vietnam-era SEAL, Lyon's Lope is another anticipated, dreaded evolution of Hell Week. The crews race a measured one-mile course with the boats on their heads. Back in the water without boats, the crews form caterpillar-like daisy chains and stroke back and forth around the eastern end of the base. Sometimes the human chains use boat paddles; sometimes they paddle with their hands. The water temperature out in the bay is about 56 degrees.

After Lyon's Lope, the trainees begin an evolution called the base tour. They will run around the base for the next two hours with only two water breaks—one to drink and one to get wet and sandy. For many in 228, the base tour is the worst they will suffer during this long and punishing night. More than a few will call this the worst night of Hell Week. By dawn 20 men are left in Class 228.

Once the boat crews have safely made their rock portage, they hit the beach for more physical training drills with the inflatable boats. The activity dries the men out and allows them to shake off some of the cobwebs that come with the long and sleepless hours. By this time of the afternoon, most of the men are moving along well. Their stomachs know that chow time is close and they may be able to sit for a few minutes of rest and drink warm coffee.

In a seemingly never-ending series of drills, the crews make a measured mile run down the beach with boats on their heads. Timing, coordination, and the blind following of their leader keep most of the crews on track. There is no punishment for the last boat crew this time, but each of them must hit the surf after the run. A few have had enough and ask permission to ring the bell.

Tuesday is one long day of beach games, a surf passage, a run-paddle-run routine, and a drill in which trainees drag their boats through the O-course. As always, it pays to be a winner. When the trainees show spirit, the instructors reward them. When they finish a race last or start to feel sorry for themselves, the staff comes down on them. The day shift has a special treat for losers. In the back of Great White, the white pick-up truck driven by the instructors, is an IBS full of ice and water. Losers or trainees who show poor spirit are sent for a quick dip through the cold slurry. Most of them have now been up for more than 56 hours. They're in a mental fog, yet they must physically keep moving. One man doesn't, and the class is cut to 19.

After evening chow, the three remaining boat crews do their elephant walk, boats bow to stern, back to the special warfare center and to medical for a hygiene check. To one degree or another, most of them have swollen joints and multiple abrasions. Many are starting to develop a bald spot on top of their heads from the boats. Their knees are beginning to swell, and some of them are limping as they run and shuffle from one evolution to the next.

Tuesday night's drill will begin with a boat cache and escape and evasion (E&E). After the two-and-a half-mile paddle to North Island, the trainees cache the boats and are divided into pairs. They are sent on a run north for a half mile to the main lifeguard tower

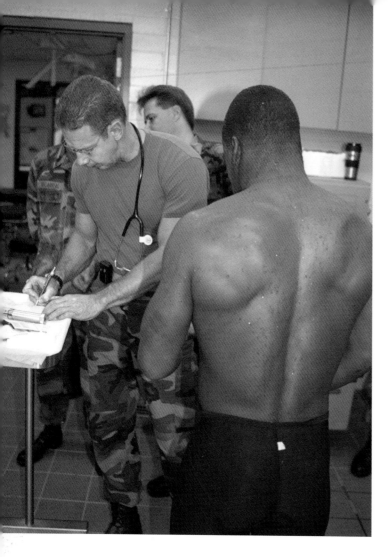

A quick medical inspection follows a morning trip through the obstacle course. The men have slept only a few hours and are happy to rest a few minutes during the examination. Surprisingly few serious injuries are found, although the men limp around like refugees from a hospital ward. Among the problems are swelling in the knee joints and minor scrapes. All are pronounced fit to continue their adventure through Hell Week.

on the North Island recreational beach. From there they have to make their way back to the boats and trucks while avoiding the instructors who are out looking for them. It's a grand game of hide and seek. This is another traditional Hell Week evolution, and the evading pairs all have their own ideas on how to beat the instructors. But it really doesn't matter which pairs are caught and which aren't. Everyone ends up cold, wet, and sandy.

After the E&E exercise and a short period of surf torture, the three boat crews begin paddling south from North Island for Silver Strand State Park some six miles down the coast. The trainees have quickly learned that when they are paddling, they don't have to put up with harassment from the instructors. If it's a long paddle, they have a chance to dry out. Except for the pain of not being a winner, the three-boat regatta has little incentive to make the paddle swiftly.

Medical corpsmen take a close look at every man in the class during one of several scheduled examinations. Many of the trainees have cuts, scrapes, and scratches that need cleaning and medication. Crotch rot is the most common problem, which is caused by the constant trips into the wet surf and sand dunes. Most abrasions aren't real problems early in the week, but after hours upon hours of dirt and grime, even the smallest scratch can become infected if ignored. More serious injuries always get immediate attention.

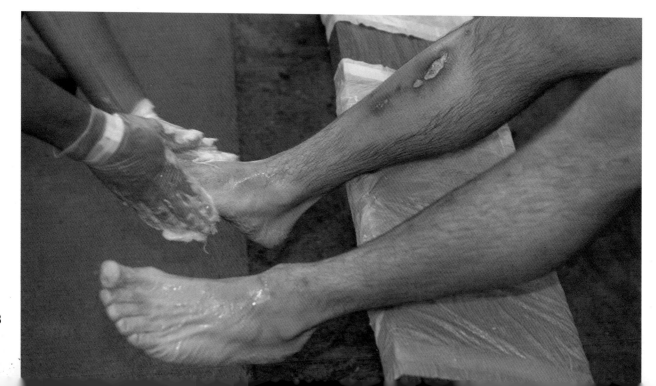

Covered with mud, the trainees take part in one of the most notorious events of Hell Week. Their "trial by mud" consists of some games and swims in the mud flats of San Diego Bay. Swim buddies have to hold hands or will lose their partner because few can see more than a few inches. Punishment might be making a mud angel or pulling your partner through the muck and grime. Soon it becomes a game for the tired men.

Once the class has gotten completely covered with mud, it is ordered to play a series of games. Mindless things like leapfrog, relay races, wheelbarrow races, and mud swim races have become difficult. After about an hour, the two-man teams quickly learn that a game winner gets to hit the surf. While the water might be cold, the water is a welcome refreshment that gives the trainees a few moments of being clean and somewhat less stinky.

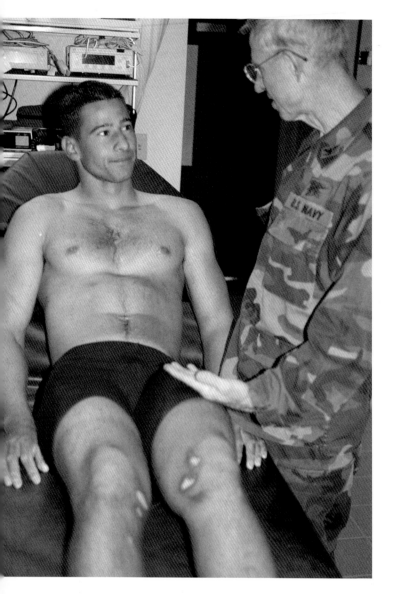

As Hell Week takes its toll on the class, a senior Navy doctor examines each man. The doctor talks quietly as he carefully looks for physical injuries. Most of the men will not admit to having any physical problems that a little sleep wouldn't cure. None seem to be having any mental problems understanding where they are and what's happening.

Upon arriving at the state beach, four miles south of the special warfare center, the three boats cross over the Silver Strand Highway to the San Diego Bay side and the mud flats. Trial by mud has been a part of Hell Week since the days of the first frogmen who trained in the mangrove swamps near Fort Pierce, Florida. There are boat crew races, wheelbarrow races, relay races, leapfrog races, fireman's-carry races, races in which the men crawl on their stomachs, and races where they wriggle along on their backs. They make mud angels facedown on their stomachs. This is dirtywork but relatively harmless. Winners get a few moments' respite from the mud. Losers race again.

No matter how tired they are, the trainees always compete, trying for a break from the misery or a chance to rest for a moment. At first, this seems like mindless harassment, but it is part of the sorting process, a method to identify those who have a will to win under any conditions. The Vietnam-era SEALs recall the mud flats as training wheels for combat patrols in the rice paddies and mangrove swamps of the Mekong Delta. Mud games last an hour and a half. The class is then sent into deeper water to wash off enough of the mud so that it can get into the chow hall. Following the wash-down, the trainees paddle north along the west shoreline of the bay to return to the base.

After breakfast, it's again back to the special warfare center for hygiene inspection. The Hell Week class has been checked morning and evening by the medical staff, but now the clinic medical officers are inspecting them very closely. In spite of the antibiotics all trainees received before Hell Week began, their immune systems are struggling. By Wednesday morning, most of them have been up for three full days with no sleep. The two doctors and their physician's assistant are alert for a host of problems, not the least of which could include an outbreak of flesh-eating bacteria.

The medical inspection is a gauntlet of sorts, much like what happens when a race car comes in for a pit stop. First, the trainees strip to their shorts in the outside shower at the barracks and wash off the top layer of mud and dirt. After they get spritzed with a disinfectant, they scrub themselves down with antiseptic scouring pads. The cold trainees get a brief taste of hot water followed by a cold shock as they stand before hall fans to dry off. They then pad over to the clinic, where they queue up to be inspected by one of the three medical officers.

The medical officers are meticulous and quick. They inspect the trainees' hands, feet, and genitals, and carefully listen to their chests. All the while, they ask questions. Some trainees will admit to problems; others won't. Often the doctors have to be detectives as well as physicians. A few of the trainees are allowed ibuprofen, but the medical staff does not dispense it freely.

Very few moments are available for any sleep or rest during Hell Week. Boat crews that finish fast are allowed a moment to close their eyes, while the slower ones finish. Instructors are content to allow some of this rest but will quickly send any man who is sound asleep into the surf. The smarter crews will appoint one man to keep watch during each drill, while the others take a rest.

Toward the end of Hell Week most of the class members are like walking zombies. Their eyes are all nearly shut and every part of their body is wet and tired. All have learned to rest without sleeping whenever an opportunity comes along. Some seem to be sleeping with their eyes open. Each man knows the week's end is nearing. Each man also knows that "the only easy day was yesterday."

After they leave the exam room, the trainees pause to swab their crotch and groin areas with a vitamin A and D ointment. Most pull on one of the available cloth penis socks that will help with the sand and chaffing. They leave the clinic through the side door, where more medical personnel are waiting for them. One at a time, the trainees step through an ice-water bucket in their bare feet and take a seat on a picnic table. A corpsman sprays their feet with a disinfectant, another swabs them with a topical silicon gel, and they're done. Good to go for another round of Hell Week.

Next to the picnic table is a line of milk crates, one per trainee. Each has a change of dry clothes. And, for a brief moment, they are warm and in dry clothes. But just around the corner is an instructor

Now the boat crews are so tired that half the men hold the boat on their heads, while the others simply hang on to their strap and get dragged along the beach. Instructors keep an eye out for this activity and reward it with a crew trip into the surf. By now everyone is wet and half asleep. The few remaining days of Hell Week seem like months away as the trainees slowly move down the beach. Leaders emerge and keep their crews motivated and awake.

Boat crews move through the obstacle course with their small inflatable boats, surmounting each barrier more by memory than by sight. They keep each other moving and awake with shouts aimed at beating their fellow crews. Winners get a rest this time, while losers hit the surf with their boat. There are shouts of "hoo-ya," and then a few moments' rest before the next challenge is presented by the instructors.

from the day shift, ready and waiting with a water hose to wet them down. Next is a trip across the beach and into the surf. Then a roll on the beach and 228 is again cold, wet, and sandy.

How much sleep trainees get, and when, varies from one Hell Week to another. Class 228 will be given a total of five hours of scheduled sleep during its Hell Week. After noon chow, the instructors send the trainees to the one remaining tent for their first sleep period. The class has shrunk enough that the second tent is no longer needed. Inside the remaining tent, the air is damp and heavy with stale sweat. Some fall asleep immediately. Others have fought to stay awake so desperately that their bodies will not turn off. They simply lie on their cots staring mindlessly at the canvas ceiling. A few sit and doze, or they walk around afraid that if they give themselves over to sleep, they will lose the courage to get up and keep going.

"Fweeeeet!" A long whistle breaks the silence. Their hour-and-a-half sleep period is over. "Let's go! Let's go! Time to hit the surf!"

Inside, a few trainees simply rise and stagger to the tent opening. Others bolt upright, wide awake but totally confused. It takes a few moments for them to break through their dazed condition and to figure out where they are. Once reality sinks in, they drag themselves from their cots to shuffle after their classmates. Still others need to be called back from the dead. They rise like zombies, unsure of what's happening, but somehow knowing that they must be up and moving. More surf torture and more beach games follow.

After the evening hygiene inspection at the pool, they have pool games and, for a change, warm water. The instructors direct 228 in a game of king of the hill, or king of the boat. The trainees fight for who can stay in the small inflatable boat or who gets tossed over the side.

After pool games, the class dresses and rigs the boats for land travel. For the rest of Wednesday and well into Thursday morning, Class 228 carries the boats up and down the beach. When the trainees can barely stand, they begin surf-passage drills. At 0400 hours,

The class gets its final medical check after a quick wash-down. It's so quick that there isn't any time to rest. Everyone is in good spirits and physical shape, considering they can't remember the last time they got some sleep. Each man does his best to convince the others, and himself, that the end is near. They tell each other the last of Hell Week is easy. But it never is.

the men begin their second sleep period. This time they sleep on the beach for an hour and a half. For those claimed by sleep, the awakening is agony. For those who doze, it's just a return to the reality of Hell Week.

Back under the boats, they struggle across the base to the chow hall for breakfast and back to the special warfare center for morning hygiene check, a two-mile round trip. The medical staff gives them another thorough inspection. This is the last full-on medical class inspection until the class finishes Hell Week. It's now Thursday, and the sun is up on the next-to-last day. It will be a very long day.

The class returns to the main part of the naval amphibious base and parks its boats on Turner Field, the base soccer field. The instructors divide the class

into two teams and set them upon each other in a soccer match. It's a surprisingly hard-fought and intense game. The trainees are groggy and half dead on their feet, but they're still competitors. Some have played soccer before and some haven't. Spirit counts as much as skill. But it's an active game, and the warmth of the California sun gives Class 228 a chance to dry out. After the noon chow, they walk the boats back to the beach near the O-course.

The next evolution is stretch physical training. The shift instructor puts the men through a quick regime of serious stretching exercises, then through some not-so-serious ones, such as eye openers and eyebrow stretches. When the nearby instructors begin to laugh, the class realizes a joke has been made about its weariness. It's Thursday afternoon of Hell Week, and the instructors are just trying to keep the trainees awake, on their feet and moving. After a round of beach games, the class is sent to its tent home on the beach for the third and final sleep period. Even though their bodies are desperate for sleep, most of them fight it, not wanting to suffer the agony of waking up. Some lie down only to rest, and sleep claims them immediately. Others sit on the side of a cot and doze fitfully. They know it's their last sleep period, and almost their last day of Hell Week. Deliverance is less than 24 hours away.

A few BUD/S trainees go through Hell Week, take what comes, and never consider quitting. They know what they want and will pay the price. Unless they get hurt, they'll make it or die trying. But most trainees, at one time or another, become weary enough to question their stamina and their ability to endure this training. This may cause them to ask themselves if they really belong here. A few experience a real personal crisis. They ask themselves: "Is this what I really want to do? Is it really worth all the pain and the cold and the lack of sleep to be a Navy SEAL?" Some get past it; some don't. But most who make it to Thursday afternoon will not quit. They may get hurt or sick, but they will not quit.

The last sleep period is shattered by whistles, and Class 228 is back in the Pacific Ocean—cold and wet and back in Hell. The two-mile round trip to chow is agony, and the trainees stagger under the boats trying to keep it together. In the chow hall, they try to encourage each other, but many begin to slump into their food trays.

Happy to be paddling through the mild surf because they can go slowly and rest a little, boat crews make their way in an "around-the-world paddle." It's the last major evolution in Hell Week, and they can see the end. It will, however, be the longest night they experience in the week. They paddle along the surf line to the Hotel del Coronado, around North Island, and through the ships at anchor. After that, it's back to the Silver Strand for a quick trip to the chow hall. One more long day.

Boat crews sit and wait for the sun to set along the beach at the amphibious base. Most are too tired to remember everything that happened during Hell Week, but they know it's only one long day until it's all over. They have completed what will be the most difficult week in their life outside of combat. They will come to learn, as SEAL team operators, that Hell Week was just a small sample of what they will face in real combat situations. But in combat, the enemy will be watching instead of the instructors.

Boat crews slow in returning from a water drill get special attention. Instructors keep their students holding boats above their heads for several minutes. Each crew wants to be the last to drop in pain, which earns them a little rest while the others hit the surf again.

"C'mon, man, stay awake."

"Hang in there, we're almost home."

"Hey, it's almost Thursday night. It is Thursday, right?"

"Thursday! We get through tonight and it's done."

After a wash-down at the clinic and a quick hygiene check, they begin the around-the-world paddle. Everyone in the class is battered, but one of the officers is in the worst shape. He cannot bend one of his legs because his knee is the size of a football, and he still has fluid in his lungs. He begs the doctors to let him continue. Since the remainder of Hell Week

will, for the most part, be in the boats rather than under them, he joins his boat crew for the big paddle.

By tradition, the around-the-world paddle is the last major evolution in Hell Week. Many will remember this as the longest night of their lives. But lurking deep in the fog of their semiconsciousness, they know it's the last night. Knowing that there will be an end to their pain and suffering is almost too delicious to think about.

They enter the water at the naval special warfare center at 1930 hours and paddle the boats north along the west shore of Coronado. It's a long journey around Coronado, made longer by the instructors who periodically call them ashore, feed them, and put them through surf torture. The men paddle around the rock jetty that marks the entrance to San Diego Bay and east toward the lights of the city. By 0300 they have cleared the north end of Coronado and the naval air station and are paddling south. By 0400 three of the smallest crafts in the Navy pass one of the largest as they stroke by the USS *John C. Stennis* (CVN 74), a 1,092-foot, 98,000-ton aircraft carrier. They make it to the boat ramp at the amphibious base shortly after 0500. There is still no sign of dawn as the exhausted trainees rig for land travel and take the boats to a head carry. The chow hall is only a few hundred yards from the boat ramp at Turner Field. For the men under the boats, it seems like several miles.

The men of Class 228 know it's Friday. They talked about it on the around-the-world paddle. Yet they're vulnerable to anything someone tells them, even if it's unreasonable. When the instructors tell them it's Thursday morning, they have to think about it. They're starting to have memory lapses. While standing, they can drift off for a few seconds, and when they snap back awake, it takes them a moment to reconnect. They file into the chow hall like the walking dead.

There is undisguised pity on the faces of the food service workers as the trainees stumble past them on Friday morning. "Eggs? Pancakes? Hash browns?" they ask.

Decisions like this are hard and require energy and concentration. Most just nod and take what's given them. They line up at the drink dispenser, for there is immediate warmth there. Most take several cups of hot water. When they reach the tables, they immediately wrap their hands around a cup for warmth. Some pause to dump in packets of hot chocolate mix; others simply sip and blow at the hot water.

After morning chow, Class 228 is back on San Diego Bay. The three weary crews head down the bay, each trying to maintain a stroke count. Some fall asleep paddling and have to be roused by their crew mates. But gradually, as the dawn swells to daylight, each is becoming more aware that this is Friday. The last day. It's a powerful concept for the 19 survivors of Class 228—Friday. The men drift into a mental fog for a moment and then snap back out. Friday is still there—

Standing at attention in the warm sun may be the only rest this trainee gets during a long Hell Week. Many of the men learn to sleep in this position, although they risk getting caught and punished with a run into the cold surf.

the last day. The instructors are waiting for them at Fiddler's Cove Marina. More beach games, cold water, and boat races are to come. Finally, they are moving down the sand road that leads westward from the cove across the Silver Strand. Once they are across the highway, they park their boats by the entrance to a small chain-link compound. So Sorry Day is about to begin.

CHAPTER 4
SO SORRY DAY

Trainees crawl along a simulated combat trail filled with barbed wire, green smoke, and the blank rounds of automatic weapons flashing overhead. So Sorry Day is an endless encounter with demolition blasts, dirt, and muck that's even worse than the mud flats. While each man knows this is the last set of trials, he is tired and frustrated at every turn. This is a true test of how the men will react in combat, and each exercise will be more difficult than the last.

Two teammates maneuver through low-lying wire on the So Sorry Day course. In order for a man to navigate the So Sorry Day course and pits, he will need help from his teammate. The noise of explosions and weapons fire, accompanied by the shouts of instructors, make verbal communications nearly impossible. Teams use hand signals when encountering an obstacle, but few signals are needed at this point of the training. The teams have worked through every part of training together, and each man knows instinctively how his teammate works.

So Sorry Day has its origins back in the early days at Fort Pierce, where the first demolition trainees were exposed to demolitions and simulated combat conditions. They were forced to crawl under barbed wire and through mud while live explosions were set off around them. The half-pound blocks of TNT that were used to create the explosions for So Sorry Day at Basic Underwater Demolition/SEAL (BUD/S) training have since been replaced by artillery simulators. In deference to the local ecology and the sea bird population on the Silver Strand, TNT is no longer used. Even so, as Class 228 crawls into the demo pits, its members are about to be treated to an evolution laced with noise, gunfire, and tradition.

Demo pits is a misnomer, as the "pits" is a single oval hole dug into the sand that is served by several culverts. The pit measures perhaps 100 feet on the long axis. During Hell Week, sea water is pumped into this hole to a depth of six or seven feet. The man-sized culverts buried into the berm that surrounds the pit allow the trainees to crawl into and out of the pit.

Members of Class 228 begin their journey into the demo pits by crawling under a field of barbed wire just inside the gate. Their vision is cut by thick smoke from smoke grenades, which also produce a strong stench of sulfur. Artillery simulators on either side of the field of barbed wire start their whistle and boom. Then the M-43s begin to bark. So Sorry Day is underway. The trainees approach the end of Hell Week just as they began, with plenty of shooting and explosions. The noise is not so bad as it was in the enclosed grinder of the BUD/S compound, but the smoke adds another element to the chaos. With two blasts on the whistle, the men crawl on their bellies. With one blast, they cover up. More shooting and explosions follow.

For the better part of an hour, the SEAL hopefuls crawl under barbed wire, through smoke, and in and out of the pit by way of the concrete culverts. A thick layer of scum has formed on the surface of the pit from the reaction of sea water and freshly dug sand. The students are past caring or questioning as they half swim, half slither through the pit, occasionally shouting encouragement to each other. They are fairly sure that the end of Hell Week is not too far off. Yet they are very, very tired and not thinking clearly. The only thing they do know is that they have to keep moving and do what is asked of them, whatever that may be. Suddenly they are called from the demo pits and sent to their boats.

"Let's hit the beach, men," an instructor shouts, "Time for you guessed it, surf passage!"

The instructors send the trainees, once again, into the cold surf. The trainees are starting to lean on each other, and two trainees have to help the ensign with the swollen knees into the water. They resemble stiffly animated rag dolls. They are made to lie in the surf and begin a series of flutter kicks. The instructors watch them carefully and professionally, with no sense of pity for their suffering. They know it's a hard business, one that demands hard men. The shift senior instructor calls the trainees in from the ocean, and the First Phase officer motions them to gather around him and announces: "Okay, men. The next evolution is, well . . . there is no next evolution. Hell Week is over. You are secured."

There is a pause while the survivors of Class 228 take this announcement in. At first they suspect this is some sort of deception, and they wait a moment for the other shoe to drop.

"Congratulations," the officer adds. "You guys did a helluva job. I'm proud of you."

"It's over?"

"Really—no bullshit?"

"Hey, man, it's over!"

"Oh, God! Oh, dear God!"

"That's it! We're secure!"

"We did it! Sonnovabitch, we did it!"

"It's really over. We're really secure!"

The entire class crawls through a series of cement tubes, while simulated gunfire zips overhead. The passages are just wide enough for a knee-banging crawl by a single man. There is so much dirt and smoke in the culvert that the first man must feel his way along. One by one, his teammates grab onto a leg in front of them and get pulled into the darkness. One of the tubes is often blocked, requiring the team to back out and find another passage; that team will not reach the pits first.

"Yeessss!"

"Hoo-yah!"

Some grasp their deliverance quickly; for others, it takes a few stunned moments. Slowly, the 19 remaining members of Class 228 begin to hug each other and hoarsely cheer their survival and fellow-ship. Some are in shock and just stand there with a goofy grin on their face. A few weep with joy that the torment and the cold are over. One drops his head a moment, crosses himself, and then goes about shaking each of his classmate's hands.

It is Friday, November 19, and Hell Week is over for Class 228.

Hell Week is a curious and unique event. I'm not sure I understand it much better now, having just watched it, than when I went through my Hell Week some 30 years ago. I do know that it changes a man forever. Future challenges and many of life's triumphs are now calibrated by this experience. For a few souls, Hell Week is their zenith, and they have a difficult time getting past it. For them, making it through Hell Week is the end goal. But for most BUD/S trainees, it is a learning experience and becomes a powerful engine for future physical and mental growth.

When Draper Kauffman first began to train the naval combat demolition units (NCDUs) in the summer of 1943, he visited the naval scouts and raiders training camp, then co-located at Fort Pierce with the NCDUs. He took their eight-week physical conditioning program and compressed it into a single week of training. This first week was called "Indoctrination Week," but it quickly became known as Hell Week. The theory behind this grueling initial week was to weed out the weak ones early on and train those who remained. Since then, Hell Week has been moved from the first week of training to several weeks into it.

This "train-the-best, discard-the-rest" philosophy was not the only legacy of Draper Kauffman. He and his officers went through the first Hell Week with their NCDU enlisted volunteers. The idea that officers have to train and suffer with their men, especially suffering of this magnitude, is unique in American military service. Today, officer trainees, like SEAL platoon officers, have to lead while under pressure and have to suffer the same hardships as their men. SEAL work is a harsh, physically demanding business. If an officer is to lead from the front, he needs to be, at a minimum, as physically capable as the men he expects to follow him.

After negotiating the first lane of barbed wire, explosions, and cement tubes, the class is in for another unpleasant surprise: the pits of Hell Week. Measuring about 100 feet long by 25 feet wide, the seven-foot-deep pit is full of sand, salt water, and slime from the beach. Dropping into the pit makes getting wet and sandy seem like visiting one of the spas in the nearby Hotel del Coronado. The men's groans can be heard over the constant explosions.

Staying afloat in the slimy pits, the class must take a quick head count to account for every man. The instructors will often hold a man back at the cement tubes, requiring a team to make a quick search and find the man before an instructor asks the senior officer or petty officer for an accounting of the class. Losing a man would be a serious safety violation, but the class has worked as a team for so long it has no problem knowing when a man is slow reaching each target.

The history of Hell Week is a microcosm of the history of the SEAL teams. As an organization, the Navy SEALs force is quite young, just a little more than 40 years old. The SEALs' evolutionary cousins, the Navy frogmen, have yet to turn 60. Both the frogmen and the SEALs were born out of necessity, as was Hell Week. The slaughter of young Marines on the beaches of Tarawa underscored the need for beach reconnaissance prior to amphibious landings. Volunteers for this dangerous work had to be recruited and trained quickly. Hell Week quickly became the crucible—a fast way to find the right kind of men for this task. They were hastily organized and rushed overseas to clear

After a refreshing trip into the nearby surf, each man must maneuver over the pits on a makeshift rope bridge. If one man falls, his teammate must jump in and save him. As punishment, the entire class gets another opportunity to cross. After several attempts, every man makes it safely across, and a huge shout of "hoo-yah" erupts from the class. As a reward, the class gets to do a surf passage in the boats. The men are so tired they can barely lift the boats.

With guns and simulated rockets blazing overhead, a Hell Week trainee crawls into the smoke, dirt, and barbed wire. By now he has been through the course several times and knows to keep his head down and keep moving. The rest of his class is close behind, each man grabbing the pant leg of the one ahead as a means of reaching the end at the same time. Everyone makes it through the course. The week's end is near.

the obstacles for the amphibious landings at Sicily. Those who went ashore to clear the beaches at Normandy for the D-Day invasion suffered terrible casualties. On Omaha Beach alone, 52 percent were killed or wounded.

The NCDUs were consolidated into underwater demolition teams (UDTs) shortly before the end of the war. As UDTs, these first American frogmen saw action across the Pacific as American forces fought their way from island to island on the way to Japan. A few years later in Korea, they served with distinction, raiding coastal targets and performing critical hydrographic reconnaissance prior to the landings at Inchon. Throughout the war in the Pacific and the Korean War, the Navy frogmen were defined by what they had endured during Hell Week.

January 1962 marked the commissioning of SEAL Team One in the Pacific fleet and SEAL Team Two in the Atlantic fleet. Training SEALs, like training frogmen, demanded a rigorous Hell Week. The new SEALs focused on duties that included unconventional warfare, operational deception, counterinsurgency, and direct-action missions in maritime and riverine environments.

During the Vietnam War, SEAL direct-action platoons and advisor teams compiled an impressive record of combat success. At the height of the conflict, no more than 500 Navy SEALs were on active duty, and there were seldom more than 120 SEALs deployed in the combat zone. But these SEAL warriors were able to operate for endless hours, under very stressful combat situations. Even years later, the SEALs attribute this mental and physical strength to their training in Hell

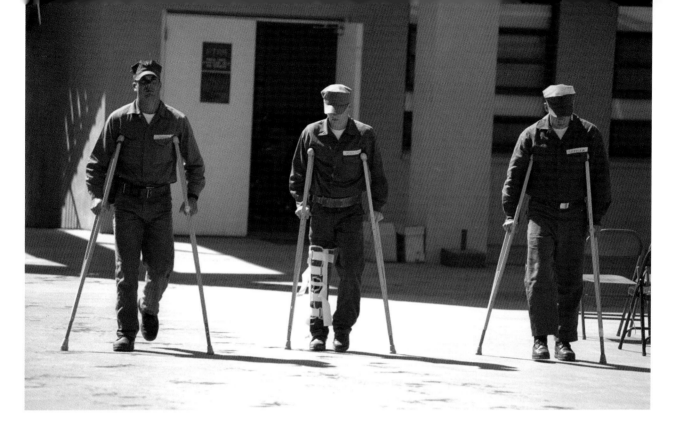

Three trainees who have suffered medical problems too serious to continue in the class make their way to a holding division. They will be examined and observed. If the injuries are not too bad, the trainee will attend classroom sessions and then get assigned to a new class. Some injuries are too serious for a man to complete BUD/S. Future assignments for these men are handled on an individual basis.

Week. Since Vietnam, changing missions and increased operational tempo have prompted the underwater demolition teams to be redesignated as SEAL teams and SEAL delivery vehicle (SDV) teams.

Hell Week and the making of Navy SEALs have become more structured since my time with Class 45. But from what I saw with Class 228, Hell Week has not become any easier.

As the dense smoke of simulated combat rises from the So Sorry Day pits, trainees and instructors breathe a collective sigh of relief. Fewer than 20 of the original men who started with the class remain. They have just completed the single most physically and mentally difficult week of training in the military. Future BUD/S training will continue to be difficult, causing more men to drop out, but nothing short of combat will ever equal what they have done in the past week.

CHAPTER 5
SECOND PHASE:

An advanced dive instructor demonstrates one of the basic tools of a Navy SEAL, the Draeger scuba rig. Named after its makers, this is a self-contained breathing unit that recirculates the diver's air without allowing any bubbles to escape to the surface. SEALs use the Draeger to reach targets silently, unseen by an enemy on the water's surface. Each Basic Underwater Demolition/SEAL (BUD/S) trainee will have several hours of extensive pool and ocean training with this equipment.

INTO THE SEA

Following in the legendary footsteps of the Navy's World War II frogmen, SEAL trainees begin their second phase of training in full scuba gear. In addition to countless hours of continued physical exercise, they will now enter the classroom and the water, learning to become frogmen themselves. Every Navy SEAL operator is an advanced scuba diver, comfortable in any sea and under most any conditions. Many of those conditions will be duplicated in this phase of training.

At 0500 hours on Monday, December 13, Class 228 officially begins Second Phase with physical training on the Second Phase grinder, a blacktop area just outside the dive locker. It is a rough workout, but nothing like the first day of First Phase. Class 228's numbers have evolved since the class finished Hell Week. Of the 19 originals who finished Hell Week, only 15 have made it to Second Phase. One quit and another three were physically unable to continue. Eleven men were added to Class 228 after Hell Week, bringing the total to 36 trainees. These were men who

had completed a previous Hell Week but needed time to heal after their ordeal.

After Hell Week in First Phase, three weeks of hydrographic reconnaissance training and more cold-water swimming are left. One of the men who just joined Class 228 does not make it.

After a run across the base for breakfast and back, the others file into the Second Phase classroom. Their schedule will keep them close to the classroom for the next two weeks. Except for room and personnel inspections, O-course runs, timed and

Phase Two starts out with a splash, as trainees don the most basic of scuba equipment and prepare to hit the amphibious base's combat pool. Trainees will spend most of the coming weeks with heavy aluminum twin-80 compressed air tanks and double-hose air regulators strapped to their backs. Including weight belts, fins, and masks, each man carries 125 pounds of extra weight. Thankfully, the men are allowed to sit while waiting for a turn in the pool with instructors.

A SEAL instructor makes notes following the safety examination of a trainee's dive equipment. Careful records are kept on each man. The class members patiently wait, with double-hose regulators in their mouths. Learning to use these has become second nature by the time the class reaches the open ocean.

Just after the trainees become competent scuba divers, the underwater harassment begins. Instructors swoop down from the surface, turning off air and removing the face masks of trainees. The men must immediately check their equipment, return it to correct operation, and continue on with their swim course. While most of the problems could easily be corrected by a teammate, this is one of the few times a man will operate alone.

conditioning runs, and timed two-mile ocean swims, they will focus on academics. The first week is devoted to diving physics, and the second is devoted to dive tables and diving medicine. The academic portion of Second Phase concludes at the end of week two. Students must pass exams in diving physics, diving medicine, and diving decompression tables. Most make it, but not all of them. Three men wash out because they cannot pass their exams. One man is an original from Class 228.

On week three, the class begins open-circuit scuba in the pool, a major test for the class. They must pass their pool competence test, which amounts

to underwater harassment, in order to continue in Second Phase. This is to see if the trainees can handle adversity underwater and not panic. It is called the Hell Week of Second Phase. Pool competence causes another 10 men from the group to fail, and the class becomes smaller. Only one of those who quits is an original member of Class 228, a solid trainee who develops a sinus condition and cannot handle the pressure at depth. The class finishes the pool competence testing with 23 men.

The open-circuit portion of Second Phase concludes with a 120-foot-deep bounce dive off Point Loma. The brief dive to the bottom and back, almost

With the exception of daily runs, swims, and a little work on the obstacle courses, trainees will spend the better part of two weeks studying in a classroom. Navy dive training is intensive, covering such diverse subjects as physics, physiology, and medicine, as they relate to being underwater. The courses are difficult, even for college graduates. Each man must pass the extensive written exams in order to continue dive training. Those who can't pass are dropped from Basic Underwater Demolition/SEAL training.

Two instructors provide substantial underwater harassment to trainees during a pool session. Not only do the instructors turn off the trainee's air tank and remove his face mask, they also twist the air regulators' hoses into knots. The trainee must learn to correct these problems, following a set of rules and routines, without rushing to the surface for air. Many consider this the most difficult portion of training in Second Phase. Several can't handle the adversity and drop out.

A huge blast of air escapes from a trainee's twin tanks after an instructor pulls a regulator hose loose. The old-fashioned double-hose regulators are used for this training so that each man is comfortable correcting any potential problem underwater. The hose must be reconnected while the man holds his breath and then clears the hose with a force of breath from his lungs. The modern single-hose regulator, which can be cleared of water by simply pushing a button, will be used in the advanced dive training.

Dive buddies assemble their equipment prior to an open-water scuba dive. Soon, each of the teams will check another team's equipment. Once the teams are ready, each man must pass an instructor's careful examination. No mistakes in procedure or use of equipment will be tolerated, and trainees take this portion of their safety inspection very seriously. Their lives depend on their equipment operating correctly and the capabilities of their dive buddy.

The men of Class 228 carefully examine their scuba equipment in preparation for their first open-water dive. Their equipment will be checked twice before every dive. A safety violation could result in being dropped from the class. A serious violation could prove fatal to an apprentice diver. Becoming a competent scuba diver is the very heart of becoming a Navy SEAL.

like a ball bouncing, is anticlimactic after their struggles in the pool. The water is clear and cold, and there is no harassment. The students are dressed in wet-suit tops and hoods. Four students and an instructor go down the descent line from the boat to a bar at the 120-foot depth. They hang there and watch the jellyfish for a few minutes and begin their ascent. At this depth, due to the pressure, their air bubbles "tinkle" rather than "burble," a distinctly different sound. Otherwise, it is a quick, painless, cold experience. Another checkmark in Second Phase.

Thirty-six students began Second Phase, and now there are 23. Among those who remain, most are solidly meeting every challenge. A few have performance deficiencies to overcome, but all are determined to make it to graduation. The balance of Second Phase will be devoted to mastering the LAR V scuba. Instructors and trainees call it by its manufacturer's name, the Draeger. It is a closed-circuit, 100-percent oxygen tank. The Draeger is the current edition of a long line of combat swimmer scubas, tracing its lineage back to crude British and Italian models developed during World War II. The diver breathes pure oxygen, and his exhalation gas is sent through a canister that scrubs away the carbon dioxide. Additional oxygen is added to the breathing gas as needed. The theory of the oxygen re-breather has changed little over the past five decades, but the design and safety devices

The Draeger scuba is a completely self-contained unit, capable of about six hours' use underwater. Because pure oxygen is recirculated in the unit, divers can only work above 32 feet. Deeper pressures will cause oxygen to become toxic and unfit to breathe by a diver. Unlike the traditional diving tanks, the Draeger is more compact, lighter, and worn on the chest instead of the back. It is very safe and dependable when used properly.

An instructor carefully examines the dive equipment of a trainee during a dive test in the combat pool. Any incorrect procedure or improper use of equipment could result in a safety violation. For such infractions, the trainee will receive a physical punishment and must repeat the swim exam. With too many safety violations, the trainee will fail the entire pool dive test. If this happens, the man will get only one opportunity to make up the exam. A second failure results in being dropped from BUD/S training.

A BUD/S trainee watches his instructor while dressed in a full dive rig. The dive mask, hood, wet suit, and air-regulator mouthpiece will become like a second skin. Each man will become more comfortable with this environment by the time he completes practice dives and classes. There will be several pool and open-water dives before the final diving examinations are given. At this point, all the exams are given on a pass or fail basis.

Mistakes made by trainees during their dive instruction are met with severe punishment. Here, a man carries two 60-pound buckets of dive filter granules while dressed in his full scuba rig. He must make a 100-foot trip fast enough to please the instructor or keep doing it until he can't walk. As usual, it's very difficult to make the instructor happy, and this man makes several trips.

Doing 20 pushups every few minutes has become a way of life for trainees in the BUD/S program. However, in the dive phase it becomes more interesting. Trainees are given punishment in full dive gear. Now pushups must be done with an extra 125 pounds while wearing a hot wet-suit top. Most of the men can manage one series of 20 pushups during an hour-long class, but few can do more. Instructors know this limitation and are quick to give trainees a second set for not following proper procedures.

An instructor closely examines a trainee prior to his first pool test dive. Each man will already have passed an inspection by his teammate, so any improper equipment use will result in both men being punished. This usually results in a penalty of 20 pushups in full dive gear. Although the dive testing is done in the pool, any improper equipment use or a violation of any rule will count against the pool test as well. Safety is one of the most important aspects of SEAL training.

Standing ready for his first open-water scuba dive, this student is an excellent example of the type man sought for Navy SEAL team training. He is young, healthy, educated, physically and mentally strong, and highly motivated to become a warrior. But at the moment, he is only thinking about the challenge and excitement of making his first dive as a future Navy frogman.

The entire class waits for instructions at the pool's side. All the men have completed their basic scuba instruction and will complete a simple swim-in-gear session. This is done to help build physical stamina for their long, open-ocean underwater swims. While there is no pass or fail for this portion of the phase, competition is fierce among the teams to be first. As always, the last-place team gets to do pushups in full dive gear.

of these scubas have undergone considerable refinement. The Draeger is a light, compact rig worn on the diver's chest. There are no telltale bubbles, and a combat swimmer has up to six hours of underwater time to complete his mission.

The Draeger is a safe rig, so long as it is properly maintained and properly prepared for the dive. It is a shallow-water scuba. Divers using the Draeger are restricted to a working depth of 30 feet. Pure oxygen can become toxic at pressures found below the 32-foot depth of two atmospheres. During the first two days of closed-circuit instruction, the class is introduced to this diving rig that will become the trainees' underwater companion in the SEAL teams. During classroom and hands-on evaluations, they learn the care and feeding of the Draeger: how to set it up for a dive, how to perform in-water procedures, and how to maintain it. In addition to these pre- and post-dive procedures, the trainees learn to recognize signs of hypoxia, an oxygen-deficient condition, in themselves or their dive buddy. Divers who are slow or unresponsive, or who display poor judgment, may be showing the first

signs of hypoxia. Unless the man receives more oxygen, unconsciousness and possibly death will follow. Divers also learn emergency procedures should these symptoms appear or their Draegers become flooded and force them to the surface. The students pay close attention. The Draeger is a reliable scuba unless the standard procedures are not religiously observed.

For the next two weeks, Class 228 dives using the Draeger. The first two dives are familiarization evolutions in the pool. Then the men begin boring holes in San Diego Bay. Each successive swim gets longer, and each swim has a new objective or new combat swimmer technique.

Once they master the Draeger during the day, they begin the night swims. They learn to calibrate their kick count, or pace, so they can judge distance on a given course. Each swim pair carries an attack board, a pie-plate-sized Plexiglas board with mountings for a compass, wristwatch, and depth gauge. The trainees take turns "driving" on a compass heading. Gradually, the class begins to learn the basic tools of the combat swimmer: the ability to swim a good line

Trainees enter the combat pool for another test of their diving skills. Each session is more difficult than the previous, and trainees cannot fall behind and expect to complete the dive phase. Fortunately, each dive team is tested separately while the others rest alongside the pool. After the morning's run and physical training, the men will take these moments of rest where and when they are able. The resting teams also will closely watch the testing so they can glean some tips on how to pass.

A team of divers discuss how they will handle an underwater problem. Most of the dive tests and swims require an equal amount of effort and thinking by each man in a team. Trainees have already learned that most of the hazards and problems encountered by scuba divers can be quickly and easily solved by having a competent dive partner. This is the final pool dive in Phase Two, as these frogmen move from the water onto the land.

of bearing and know how far you have traveled. It's underwater navigation, the same as if they were on land with a map and compass.

Week three on the Draeger is something of a gut check. Students are starting to master the basics of a combat swimmer, but they still have physical training. During one long day they have a long physical training session, run the O-course, and have two beach runs. On that single day, including runs to the mess hall, they run more than 12 miles. At night they take to the water for pace work and to swim compass courses. They conduct underwater hull inspections of patrol craft and a Navy destroyer at night. This is a steep learning curve, especially for those in 228 who, until three weeks ago, had never taken a breath underwater. With a week to go in Second Phase, the trainees are becoming frogmen.

The class is becoming smaller. It now stands at 20 men. One man has to leave for a death in the family, and another is rolled back because of an injury. A third cannot pass the four-mile run time for Second Phase and must start SEAL training over from the beginning. All three of these are from the Class 228 originals.

The final dive problem in Second Phase is a nighttime ship attack. As with many of the Draeger dives, the trainees first do it during the daylight, then repeat the same problem at night. The final problem requires that the dive pairs approach the target ship on the surface, then submerge to make their attack. Each pair must plant its marker on the ship and swim back out to the recovery point underwater.

All 10 dive pairs pass their final dive problem and move on to the third and final phase of Basic Underwater Demolition/SEAL training.

CHAPTER 6
THIRD PHASE:

A SEAL trainee takes aim down the short-shooting range, as he enters the final part of Basic Underwater Demolition/SEAL (BUD/S) training. Every man will become very proficient with a multitude of handheld weapons and will become a very good shot, moving from target to target, before the third phase of training is completed. During that phase, they also will become well acquainted with underwater demolition.

ACROSS THE LAND

The Navy trainees visit the home of great shooters at the U.S. Marine Corps base in Camp Pendleton, California. They will spend four days here, completing several strenuous shooting exercises. They will work with a variety of weapons, also learning to clean and assemble them prior to shooting. Each man must qualify with a given weapon in order to move on to the next weapon. Every man in the class does well. Competition to be the best shooter and to outshoot the Marines is serious.

Friday afternoon, February 11. Class 228 begins Third Phase—the demolitions and tactics phase. There are now 21 men in Class 228, including 20 from Second Phase and a single roll-in from a previous class. Training is divided into two segments: training at the naval special warfare center and training on San Clemente Island. During the first five weeks of Third Phase, the trainees will be at the special warfare center. This includes four days of training at La Posta for land navigation and four days at Camp Pendleton on the shooting ranges. Then the class leaves the naval warfare center for San Clemente Island and more tactics, more shooting, demolitions, and field training exercises. Ten weeks stand between these 21 men and their goal: Basic Underwater Demolition/SEAL (BUD/S) graduation.

The first thing the new Third Phase trainees do is set up their combat load, which is carried on H-gear—a canvas utility belt that is used to carry a light load of personal infantry gear and is supported by padded

The team concept follows trainees from the water onto the land. They will continue to run, shoot, and navigate the training courses as two-man teams. While the physical exercise will also continue on a rigorous daily basis, every man is now in the peak of condition and has no difficulty. Physical punishments will be rare.

Moving from target to target, this BUD/S trainee shoots from the prone position. The distant target must take a direct hit before the man can move to the next position. Shooters may use as many bullets as necessary to hit a given target, and at the beginning it often requires four or five. But by the time they leave the mountain training facility at La Posta, most of the shooters are moving much faster and hitting each target with one or two shots.

nylon suspenders. The trainees have to set up their H-gear in a prescribed manner: four ammunition pouches in front, two on either side of the front buckle catch; two canteens just behind each hip; and a personal first-aid kit in the small of the back. The only optional placement of equipment on the H-gear belt is the standard-issue combat knife. Trainees carry their combat knives on their left or right hip, opposite the side they will work their rappelling line. All metal surfaces of their personal field equipment are either painted flat black or covered with olive-drab tape to keep them from reflecting light and making noise. One of the men in Class 228 is a former Marine. He

helps his classmates adjust their H-setups so that they fit properly and ride comfortably.

The Naval Special Warfare Group One Mountain Training Facility at La Posta is a rugged military reservation in the Laguna Mountains some 80 miles east of San Diego. It's used by the West Coast SEAL and SDV teams and BUD/S classes. La Posta is a Spartan facility with good shooting ranges, old barracks, some highly difficult mountain terrain, and a challenging land navigation course.

At La Posta the class learns more about patrolling, camouflage, and stealth—first in daylight, then patrolling at night. La Posta is at a 3,500-foot elevation, so the February nights are cold. Sometimes the class is allowed in the barracks with sleeping bags. Other times the men find a position in the bush. Each morning they have a killer physical training session or a conditioning run. The Third Phase tactics instructors are in excellent physical condition as a group, perhaps the best conditioned of all the BUD/S phase instructors. They lead physical training and the conditioning runs as a team. The days are spent scrambling over the Laguna Mountains. The land navigation practical test takes two days. Trainees, armed with map and compass, negotiate different courses, usually 5,000 meters in length with each leg 1,000 meters or more. Some pairs finish more quickly than others, but they all finish and they all pass the navigation practical test.

Late on Friday afternoon, February 25. Class 228 is back at the special warfare center. Earlier that morning, Class 227 graduated 26 and sent them to the SEAL teams. On Monday, members of Class 228 check out their assigned personal weapons from the armory for the week of shooting at Camp Pendleton.

Camp Pendleton is a 125,000-acre Marine Corps base between San Diego and Los Angeles. The base enjoys 17 miles of southern California coastline, which makes it one of the most developmentally desirable parcels of land in the United States. Time at Camp Pendleton is all about weapons safety and qualification and learning to be proficient with the M-4 rifle. In the SEAL teams, SEALs choose from a variety of rifles, handguns, and submachine guns, but the basic

Navy SEAL physical exercise programs continue on a rugged pace throughout the BUD/S training. In Third Phase, men move quickly from exercise to exercise, following the examples set by their instructors. All of the physical training is done as a team now, with little need for any verbal communications or punishment. The men have done so many training exercises it has become second nature. They will continue with individual and team physical programs throughout their SEAL careers.

A trainee shows the proper way to hold a weapon that he is not planning to shoot—with his finger off the trigger The basic rules of all handheld weapons are simple: Always consider a firearm loaded, especially during cleaning and transportation; never point weapons at anything or anyone; never put your finger on the trigger until you want to shoot; and know your target and what's behind it at all times. Navy SEALs and BUD/S trainees have an excellent safety record as a result of following these rules.

Weapon and shooting proficiency and safety tests are given at the end of the training program at Camp Pendleton. While there are a variety of weapons for a Navy SEAL to choose from, trainees must qualify with most of the selection available. Working in teams, they coach each other on the basic operation, shooting technique, assembly, and safety requirements of each weapon. Every man is easily able to recite these things verbatim during practice and testing.

weapon is the M-4, a shortened refinement of the M-16 rifle that has been a U.S. military standard since the early 1960s. It is similar to the CAR-15 in that it has a semicollapsible stock, but the M-4 has a slightly longer barrel. In addition to the care, maintenance, operation, and firing of the M-4, the trainees are drilled continually on safety. Weapons safety is as much a conscious attitude in handling a firearm as it is a set of rules and regulations. Each trainee can repeat verbatim:

1. *Consider all weapons loaded all the time.*
2. *Never point a weapon at anything you don't want to put a bullet through.*
3. *Never put your finger on the trigger unless you want to shoot.*
4. *Know your target and know what's behind it.*

There are a number of shooting drills, but first the trainees must shoot a qualifying score on a standard Navy rifle course. This requires precision shooting and marksmanship at 200 yards. They all qualify, which is not easy with a small rifle like the M-4.

Meals at Camp Pendleton, as at La Posta, are meals ready to eat (MREs) and are eaten either in the barracks or on the shooting ranges. Each day there is a physical evolution, usually a hard physical training or conditioning run. Conditioning runs at Pendleton are among the hardest to date. The trainees have to learn to run while carrying weapons and operational equipment. In addition to their H-gear and packs, the class must carry "Stumpy," a short, fat, 70-pound log with four carrying handles. The trainees take

two-minute turns running with Stumpy on these eight-mile runs. Again, the Third Phase cadre makes all the tough runs with the class. The physical harassment is less than it was in Second Phase but is still part of the training. Safety infractions or weapons-handling discrepancies are carefully noted by the instructors. These accumulate and have to be worked off with pushups and additional physical training.

In addition to the range work with the M-4 rifle, each trainee has to pass a weapons assembly exam. This is a bench test in which the men must disassemble and reassemble the M-4, the 9mm Sig Sauer

Navy SEALs have a wide variety of weapons available for their operations. Smaller handguns, rocket launchers, grenade launchers, and similar lightweight weapons are among the first choice for advanced operators. SEALs receive extensive testing and training on such weapons. The M-4, a shorter version of the popular M-16 automatic rifle of the Vietnam era, is the basic weapon for BUD/S training. However, firing a rocket launcher like the one pictured is one of the most popular activities in weapons training.

pistol, and the M-43 machine gun, naming each part as they go. They do this with an instructor standing by with a stopwatch. He questions them while they work: "What is the cyclic rate of fire of this weapon? What is the maximum effective range of this weapon? What is the muzzle velocity of this weapon?"

Class 228 then moves on to SEAL tactical shooting exercises. These are drills in which the trainees run between the shooting stations, each of which is different: a trash can, a vehicle, and a window frame. They learn combat shooting techniques, such as how to roll on their sides to shoot from under a car or the best way to take a brace on a window sill. Their targets are metal silhouettes, which ping when hit. The trainees race from station to station, double-tapping (shooting twice) each target. The target silhouettes

vary in range from 50 to 100 meters. The students' scores are a function of time and the number of hits. As with many combat skills, smooth skills equal speed.

One of the final drills at Camp Pendleton is the class "top gun" shoot off. This is a single-elimination tournament with two shooters going head to head on the range. Each has a magazine and 10 rounds locked into his M-4 rifle and is standing at the ready position. When the senior instructor says, "Go," the two shooters drop to a kneeling position and shoot at a metal silhouette 25 meters away. Then they continue down to a prone position and shift their fire to a silhouette at 50 meters. They can fire as fast and as many rounds as they like. An instructor is standing behind each trainee as a safety observer and scorer. The first shooter to get a ping on each target wins; the other is eliminated. The

Using an M-4 rifle, a trainee attempts to pass a shooting test and a bench test against the stopwatch. Each trainee is required to recite such things as the rate of fire and muzzle velocity accuracy at a given distance while they shoot. Similar questions must be answered while a trainee disassembles and reassembles the weapon. A wrong answer generally results in beginning the exercise again. Trainees must know the weapon well enough to work quickly, almost without thinking. This is a serious business, and there are no trick questions.

Shooting proficiency testing also has evolved into a "top gun" contest between teams and individuals. Two men go head to head in a shooting course, with each man having a set number of targets, shooting positions, and bullets. While they can use as many bullets as necessary to hit each target, using more than a single shot on each target will force them to change magazines along the way. Instructors score each shooter for accuracy, speed, and safety. In addition to bragging rights, the winner gets a break on the next round of physical training.

smoothest and fastest in Class 228 is an ensign from Montana who hunted elk before he went to the naval academy with the goal of becoming a Navy SEAL.

These apprentice warriors are beginning to master the techniques of shooting. For now, the targets are numbered, concentric circles on the target ranges. On the combat ranges, they are paper or metal silhouettes. The trainees are too hard-pressed with the

pace of BUD/S to think about why it is important to get rounds on the target. That will come later, when they join their SEAL platoons and begin to train for deployment to an operational theater.

Physical conditioning continues with weekly four-mile runs, two-mile swims, the O-course, and rucksack runs in the soft sand. All are doing well in Third Phase but one. He is injured in the surf and has

A trainee receives individual instruction on the firing of a weapon by a BUD/S instructor. The training is no longer aimed at removing men who aren't able to complete the rigorous programs but rather working with men who have proven they can make it. This is a time for learning safety as well as proficiency, and every man is well aware of what can happen with any improper handling of a weapon.

to be rolled back to another class. Class 228 stands at 20 men, 10 of whom are originals from day one of 228's Indoc course. The remaining 20 men all meet the Third Phase time standards for the run, swim, and obstacle courses. Just before they begin loading out for San Clemente Island, the Third Phase officer takes them on a 14-mile beach run, the longest run at BUD/S. But the men make this run in shorts and running shoes. For most in Class 228, it's been a long time since they ran in dry clothes and in something other than boots. Ahead are the combat runs and rucksack runs on San Clemente.

CHAPTER 7
SAN CLEMENTE

Working like frogmen of earlier times, the trainees prepare underwater explosive charges. In one of their final tests on San Clemente Island, seven swim teams will set charges onto seven separate underwater cement and steel obstacles. They will also attach detonation cord between all of the obstacles, their individual charges, and the beach. The ultimate blast will be one of the highlights of their time on the island.

ISLAND: THE ROCK

This is San Clemente, "The Rock," an island paradise for SEAL training. This is the final stage of Basic Underwater Demolition/SEAL training, where all of the earlier evolutions will be combined with training in explosives. This is where the class will apply its earlier training to simulated combat problems. In addition to classes on explosives and combat tactics, the training will now pit half the class against the other in competitive trials of their skills. This is where every man proves he is worthy of being a Navy SEAL.

San Clemente, which SEAL trainees refer to as "The Rock," is one of the Channel Islands off the southern California coast. It's a rugged, boulder-strewn strip of land sparsely covered with scrub grass, ice plant, and cactus—lots of prickly pear and golden snake cactus. On a clear day, Santa Catalina can be seen to the northeast.

San Clemente is young as islands go, some three million years old. There are no trees and no ground water, yet San Clemente was inhabited by early Americans some 6,000 years ago. More recently, it was used by sheep ranchers, fishermen, and smugglers until the Navy took possession of it in 1934. Since then, the southern portion of San Clemente has been used as a naval gunnery and bombing range. On the northern end of the island, the airstrip serves to train Navy pilots for touch-and-go landings prior to landing on aircraft carriers. Other than a small group of civilian workers and sailors, the indigenous population consists of gray foxes, lizards, crows, and a few rare and

No longer conducting just boat drills with the small inflatable boats, teams work against each other and the clock to meet a specific combat goal. San Clemente Island offers an excellent terrain of water, foliage, and rock for such activities. The weather here is often cooler and wetter than on the nearby mainland. However, trainees have long ago stopped being bothered by the extremes of hot and cold weather. Now they concentrate on the objective: to beat the other teams.

endangered bird species. The coastal areas and kelp beds host large populations of marine life and California sea lions. The northern tip of the island is reserved for Navy SEALs. Most of the coastline consists of rocky outcroppings and cliffs that plunge directly into the sea. The SEAL compound enjoys a protective cove with one of the island's few sandy beaches.

Basic Underwater Demolition/SEAL (BUD/S) students have been coming to San Clemente Island since the late 1950s for weapons and demolitions training. The training compound had been a blend of

tents and prefab wooden huts until the 1989 construction of Camp Al Huey, named after "Uncle Al" Huey, a Vietnam-era master chief petty officer who dedicated his life to the teams and the training of Navy frogmen and SEALs in 1989. Camp Huey is a modern facility that has the feel of a community college, with classrooms, a dormitory, and a cafeteria. But instead of laboratories and a library, there is a weapons-cleaning building, an armory, an inflatable boat storage barn, and gear-staging facilities. There are no athletic fields, but there is an obstacle course.

Training teams skirt along the smoky shore after completing a run along the island's only sandy beach. From this point on, the majority of training exercises will be under simulated combat conditions and in full combat dress. Most of the time they will include smoke, live ammunition, explosions, or similar distractions. Teams must move quickly to and from each objective in order to meet the time limits set by instructors. Slow runs will result in doing the exercise again.

It's a minicampus for apprentice warriors. San Clemente focuses on weapons, demolitions, and small-unit tactics—the basics of the SEAL trade.

As soon as Class 228 arrives at the compound, the men get a tour of the facilities and quickly settle into their "dorm," which consists of squad sleeping bays. The students arrive with their M-4 rifles, rucksacks, H-gear, a change of clothes, swim gear, and sleeping bags—the bare essentials, but everything they will need for training on San Clemente. After the evening meal, the Third Phase cadre welcomes them with a shark-attack video, showing lots of great whites hitting chunks of meat underwater. Then they jock up for a tense night-conditioning swim in the cove.

On the rocky beach of San Clemente Island, class members carry explosives across a small valley leading to their first demolition target. They will place the charges among the rocks and in the water, at the back side of the island and away from the main base. The men work with very stable explosives, such as C-4, Mk-75 hose, and bangalore torpedoes. Their main objective, as in weapons training, is learning the important procedures, rules, and safety precautions needed to work with the charges.

The island obstacle course is one of the main physical exercise events. However, the men are now all experienced in clearing the various obstacles and have no problem beating the minimum times. The competition now becomes man against man, to see who can equal or better the course records. They must also compete with the times of instructors, one of whom always seems to hold the current record.

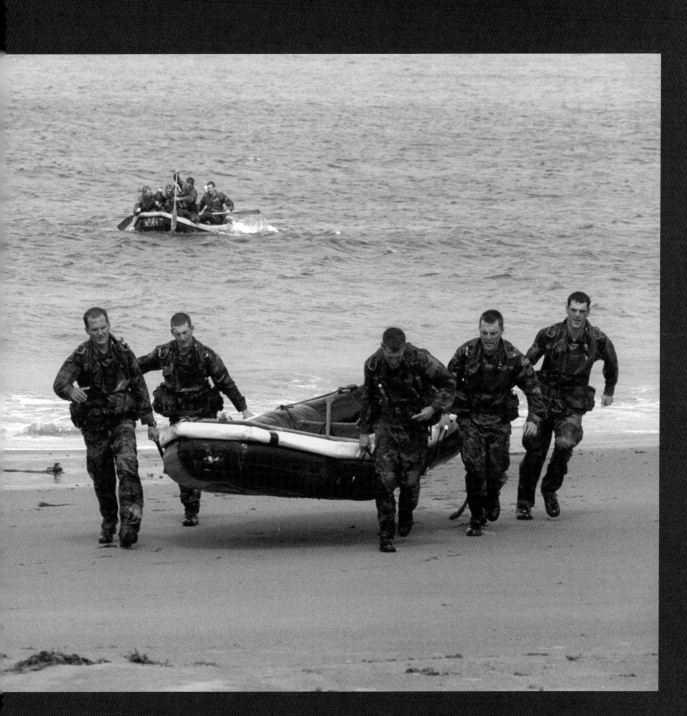

Boat teams practice beach and surf runs, landing their crafts after attacking simulated water targets. They will make several dry runs, against each other and the clock, in preparation for a real demolition objective later in the week. Every drill, in all of the BUD/S training phases, has been aimed at these few days of simulated combat. The men can feel the difference, knowing their movements as a team are directed toward a real objective. Working with live explosives and loaded weapons during the past week or two has given them a new edge of experience.

The men complete an open-water conditioning swim every day. While the objective is to keep the men in good shape, they will also be facing several under-water objectives. Each man is in excellent swimming shape and takes to the water as though it were an Olympic trial event. In the past, more than one BUD/S trainee has entered the program after being a member of the U.S. Olympic team. Several years ago, gold medalist Mike Troy completed his SEAL team training at Coronado.

Class 228 quickly learns that life on the island is different from life at the naval special warfare center. For the first time at BUD/S, the trainees eat, sleep, and live in close proximity to their classrooms and training ranges. The routines are tailored around their own facility rather than a standard naval base.

Each morning, Class 228 forms up in its compound to raise the flag and sing "The Star-Spangled Banner." The trainees form up again to lower the flag at night and sing "America the Beautiful." Their singing is coarse, off-key, and no threat to the Vienna Boys' Choir, but they get the job done. Apart from

Instructors watch over morning physical training exercises, although none of the men currently need much direction or instruction. Now they compete against the clock, doing as many repetitions of a given exercise as possible in a two-minute period. Losers don't receive any punishment, but they must endure the jeers of the other class members.

The class has learned long ago that being in good physical condition is vital to operating and surviving as a Navy SEAL. As a result, the class will do a quick series of beach pushups, or another exercise, before entering the water and moving toward an objective. The trainees will do this at their own order and not at the direction or supervision of an instructor. The pushups are no longer a punishment but part of a daily routine.

weekly runs, physical training, conditioning swims, and the O-course, the class must do "chow physical training." In the morning, the men do maximum pushups and maximum sit-ups in two-minute, timed intervals. At noon, they have to run up to Frog Rock, a pinnacle just above the camp. The distance is just a little more than 200 meters, but it's all uphill, and the last 50 meters is a steep, rocky trail. They have to make the run in less than one minute and 30 seconds. To do this, it's an all-out sprint. At night they have to do 15 chin-ups and 15 dips. All three chow physical trainings are done with full H-gear and full canteens of water.

On San Clemente, the trainees use all the weapons, demolition, and tactics instruction they received at the special warfare center, La Posta, and Camp Pendleton.

They will experience combat shooting, set off live explosives, and conduct night patrols over unfamiliar terrain—all evolutions that require planning and attention to detail.

The days are long on the island and so are the weeks. The training day begins at 0600 hours each morning, sometimes earlier, and lasts until 2000 hours, sometimes later, seven days a week. The first two weeks on the island are devoted to tactics and weapons. The weapons range at the BUD/S training camp allows for precision shooting and fire-and-maneuver drills. The trainees' precision shooting with M-4s was completed at Camp Pendleton, where they shot for qualification. At the San Clemente BUD/S range, they shoot for score with their secondary weapon, the 9mm Sig Sauer P-226 pistol.

Experienced baseball players have a definite advantage when the class trains with grenades. While throwing a grenade close to a target may seem good enough, it isn't enough for the instructors. They teach both accuracy and throwing form, never taking for granted what a near hit might accomplish. For most of the week the trainees will use dummy grenades with small, firecracker-type charges. As with most of the events on San Clemente, a furious competition to be the best develops.

After a simulated-combat beach assault, the slowest man gets to wash salt water off the weapons. Real weapons will be used for some exercises, but heavy rubber arms are used for the frequent ocean swims. While the men are used to getting dirty and sandy on a regular basis, cleanliness is stressed throughout their training. All weapons, equipment, and clothing must at least start the day in a clean and military fashion.

Class members continue to practice in shooting exercises throughout this part of training. By now most are proficient with a wide range of handguns, but the instructors are still able to provide useful tips. There will be daily shooting events and some testing, all aimed at a final qualification and proficiency simulated-combat shoot. Speed and accuracy will become the ultimate goal in this final test.

Beyond the basic marksman qualifications, the trainees have to learn to move, shoot, reload, shoot, clear jammed weapons, and continue shooting. There are performance tests for both the M-4 and the P-226. The shooting course for the P-226 emphasizes short-range shooting and speed—manipulation and marksmanship. The trainees, with their shooting coaches just a step behind them, engage silhouette targets at five to seven yards. One drill calls for them to double-tap two separate targets, center of mass, within four seconds. Another has them double-tap a silhouette, change out magazines, and double-tap it a second time within eight seconds. Smooth is fast—manipulation and marksmanship.

Performance tests with the M-4 are much the same, only the ranges are longer and the shooting more precise. From the low-ready position, the student shooters must come up to the off-hand, or standing, position and make a head shot at 25 yards within five seconds. In 12 seconds, they have to make one center-of-mass shot at 25 yards, change magazines, and make another center-of-mass shot. Then standing, they drop to the prone firing position and make two center-of-mass shots at 50 yards in 12 seconds. Shooting experience in the class varies. A few of them grew up hunting with their fathers and uncles. At least half of the trainees never fired a weapon until they joined the Navy. As the performance tests progress, the trainees of 228 gain confidence and begin putting rounds on target.

The most dangerous evolutions on the range are the immediate action drills (IADs). These drills are to SEALs what parachutes are to combat pilots. Both function as a backup for those servicemen who find themselves in grave danger. However, unlike parachutes, which are a break-glass-in-case-of-emergency item, IADs have to be learned and practiced, and they are serious evolutions. SEALs plan missions to see and not be seen—to be the ambusher, not the ambushee. But they have to be prepared if things

don't go as planned. That's why they have IADs. At BUD/S they learn the basics of IADs. Later on in SEAL qualification training, these drills will become more complex. In the platoons, SEALs will take IAD training to a very sophisticated level.

Class 228 learns two basic IADs: the leapfrog and the center peel. The leapfrog is a simple maneuver in which one element of a squad or platoon moves while the other shoots. This can be done to assault a target by leapfrogging forward, but it is primarily used to break contact by leapfrogging away. In either case, the trainees are putting live rounds downrange with men

The class is broken into two separate teams, which make their way through the grenade course. Now each man must be both fast and accurate in order to help his team emerge as the best. Each man watches as his teammate throws a grenade, willing it to land in the target circle. Winning in real combat situations, as the instructors point out, generally results in surviving.

The teams check their weapons as they prepare for a reconnaissance run across the island. Each team has a specific duty, planned earlier in the classroom, that is an integral part of the action. Instructors have revealed the basic target and desired final goal, and they will step back and allow the teams to complete the assignment on their own. The information gathered during this recon exercise will be used later for a simulated attack.

in front of them. It is critical that the fire be highly disciplined and that there be clear separation between the firing element and maneuvering element.

The center peel is a maneuver to break contact when patrolling in stagger-file order. In open country or with a larger, platoon-sized element, SEALs often patrol in two files—two lines of men moving in parallel with a stagger between the man to the left or right. The point man, who walks ahead and between the two files, encounters the enemy and engages them. He empties his magazine and initiates the center peel by running back through the center of the two files. The

two men at the head of each file shoot and peel back through the two files, changing magazines on the run. Before the trainees execute these IADs with live fire, they walk through them, then practice them on the run firing blanks. "BANG, BANG, BANG," move, change magazines. "BANG, BANG, BANG." Only then do they perform carefully choreographed, live-fire IADs.

After a week of weapons work, with the class still 20 strong, the trainees begin a block of instruction on tactics. But first the tactics instructors break them in with a rucksack run. The instructors split the class into three squads and run them around the north end

Loaded with full packs and weapons, the teams cross the water and hit the beach. They will make their way up the island, encountering several instructor-planned obstacles, to the shooting range. This is the first of their self-planned and self-motivated assaults. Their time between each obstacle and their proficiency at each obstacle will be scored. The teams move quickly and efficiently, staying within a very few points of each other.

of the island with 40-pound packs, full H-gear, full canteens, and personal weapons. Each man carries about 55 pounds for eight miles up and down hills, through cactus fields and across rock faces. Then the squads race around the airfield, another three miles, with each squad having to carry one of its members. The squads have to work as a team, distributing the "wounded" man's gear and weapons and taking turns carrying him. The three tactics instructors are loaded up like the students, and they make the run with them.

Since it always pays to be a winner, each instructor encourages his squad to finish first in the rucksack run. Navy SEALs are proud of the fact that they have never left a man behind in combat. This mindset begins here, where they learn that they can be totally exhausted and still carry a man out on the run. This is

an evolution that emphasizes teamwork, motivation, and spirit. A few in 228 are again developing stress fractures in their legs, so they are the ones carried. Distribution of the downed man's gear and the sharing of man-carry duties are essential to sustaining a good squad pace.

Following the rucksack run, the trainees hit the classroom and get down to the serious business of basic squad tactics. A key SEAL tactic they learn and will practice again and again is an over-the-beach operation (OTB). They do this once in daylight, then over and over again at night. First, they paddle to the objective area and anchor the small inflatable boats several hundred yards offshore. Then, they send in scout swimmers to survey the beach. Only then is the entire squad brought ashore.

Next, they scurry across the sand and crawl into hiding just past the high-water line. SEALs are most vulnerable when coming ashore, and they practice these sea-to-land crossings over and over in full combat gear with weapons. During over-the-beach operations, they wear fins that fit over their boots and partially inflate their life jackets to support their combat load. Once ashore, they strap the fins to their H-gear for land travel. It's cold, wet, dirty work, and it must be learned well. These future SEALs will do this again and again in advanced training and in their SEAL platoons.

Class 228 also practices basic SEAL skills such as ambushes, hasty ambushes, structure searches, prisoner handling, reconnaissance techniques, and raid planning. For the most part, they are taught to crawl, walk, and run. They learn it in the classroom, rehearse it in the field in the daylight, then go out and do it at night in simulated tactical situations. Class 228 leans into the task and works hard. The men pass their tactics and land-warfare written exams and are ready to move on to a week of demolitions.

SEAL demolitions training includes learning to use fixed ordnance, such as claymore mines and hand

An instructor watches and counts the number of shots it takes for a man to hit the distant target. In this final stage of training, each man is comfortable shooting and has little difficulty at the range. In this shoot they compete against their own earlier scores and times, hoping practice will eventually help them become an expert marksman. Most Navy SEALs are expert pistol and rifle marksmen, attributing it to the training they received at Camp Pendleton and on San Clemente Island.

Loaded with gear for combat, the men ready themselves for a night reconnaissance of their planned target. Each item of equipment, clothing, and weaponry must be double-checked by the man and his teammate. They have lived and worked with this same routine, and now it is second nature to their objective. The teams are ready for any surprises that the instructors may have waiting along the route.

Trainees carry a "dead man" and his weapons as they practice the SEAL doctrine that all casualties have to be carried home by the team. The average man carries about 50 pounds of equipment, so the added weight of a casualty must be split among the team. If a team makes a mistake during the exercise, another "casualty" may be added as a reminder of what results from errors.

After paddling to shore, the teams assault the beach in search of their target. This is the time when the men are the most vulnerable, and a point man has been sent ahead to secure the landing. Once ashore, the men still must strap on and carry their frogman fins and masks. Just like on the first day of training, the men are cold, wet, and dirty. It's a condition they will live with again and again during their careers.

Explosive satchel packs are made ready for the first underwater demolition exercise. Although supervised by instructors, the trainees must complete these preparations as a team. By this time in their training, the men are comfortable working together and the exercise moves quickly.

Trainees strap and tape a demolition hose together for a practice blast. Each hose must be properly attached to its counterpart for the proposed charge to work. While this explosive is very stable, the instructors have taught the men that no lapse in safety will be acceptable. Team leaders work with written plans, as each man takes a turn working with the materials.

grenades. Trainees also work with illumination and pyrotechnics such as pop flares and 40mm grenade-launched parachute flares. But the heart of demolitions training is the heavy demolitions: C-4 satchel charges, Mk-75 hose charges, and bangalore torpedoes. Back at the special warfare center, they learned about electric and nonelectric firing devices, charge initiation, blasting caps, and the safe handling of all these. Now it's time for the real thing. Handling explosives, like the handling of weapons, is guided by rigorous and precise standard procedures. Supervision by the Third Phase staff is constant and redundant. With the heavy demolitions, the men crawl and walk; there is no running. The trainees, as instructors closely supervise, diagram and plan the demolition shots in the classroom, then head for the range. Class 228 will get four demolition shots, three on the beach and one underwater.

The three beach shots are made with C-4 charges, Mk-75 hose charges, and bangalore torpedoes. Then the class prepares its charges for the underwater shot. Seven swim pairs prepare double Mk-138 haversacks for the seven concrete and steel beach-landing obstacles that have been positioned in 15 feet of water. Each haversack contains 25 pounds

When attached, hose charges are cumbersome and require teamwork for placement in the shallow water. Any separation of the hoses necessitates returning to the beach for repairs. Trainees quickly learn that a few extra wraps of tape will save them a half hour of additional work later. Instructors keep careful watch from a distance now, allowing the men to work as a self-contained team.

While handling explosives, the class follows a very strict set of rules and procedures. Each problem follows a series of well-planned actions that have been amply covered in the classroom. Each man knows how to do all of the separate actions required of the team.

of C-4. Because of the tamping effect that will reduce the blast, the water shot is conducted on the beach in front of the camp. Seven pairs of swimmers will load demolition shots onto the seven obstacles, and the other six trainees will circle the line of obstacles with a reel of cord to build a trunk line to connect the charges on the obstacles.

The day of the water shot, the trainees swim out to their obstacles towing their demo packs behind them. They knife the bladders that float the haversacks and follow them as they sink to the bottom. The seven pairs of swimmers begin loading C-4 on the obstacles. It's high tide, so the obstacles are in almost 20 feet of water. The men tie the explosives to their obstacles and cinch the charges in tight. The objective is close, intimate contact between C-4 and concrete. Then they tie the detonation cords into the trunk lines using knots they learned in Indoc and practiced in First Phase. The trainees have weighted themselves so they can work comfortably alongside their charges. They must perform the task without scuba tanks. Except for the fact that the water is colder and no one is shooting at them, it's like a chapter from the frogmen of World War II in the Pacific.

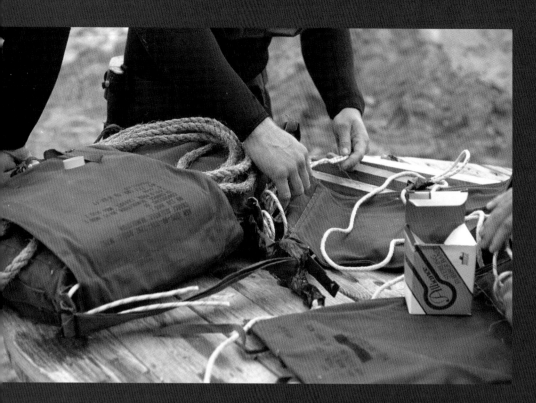

Using the same knots learned in their first phase of training, the men unwind detonation cord and head for the water to tie their charges. Placing the explosives is simply a matter of free diving to about 30 feet in the open bay and tying the package of C-4 explosive to the obstacle. Holding their breath for the minute or so, the men complete this activity with about half the effort it took in their pool training.

Working with live explosives requires close attention to the details. Every step of every action has been well rehearsed in class and with dummy charges. Even though they are closely supervised by instructors, the teams do an excellent job of preparing the charges. Although teams are responsible for their own package, each of the teams takes time to double-check the others before placement.

The trainees run from the water after placing their explosive charges, ready for the excitement of their first water blast. Instructors remain behind to closely examine every obstacle to insure there have been no mistakes. By the time the charges are set off, the explosives will have been checked at least a dozen times. The only difference in this exercise, compared to real combat, is that no one is shooting at the men.

Rising more than 100 feet into the air, this underwater blast signifies the training on San Clemente Island is nearing an end. The sound and power of the blast reverberate across the bay and islands, causing everyone in the vicinity to stop for a moment.

The class has completed the final test of Basic Underwater Demolition/SEAL training. Although the blast itself was loud and powerful, each man feels a moment of silence in reflection on the past months of training. The remaining men of Class 228 have made it through one of the toughest military training programs. And, as their instructors will tell them, their training as Navy SEALs has just begun.

Two swim pairs remain in the water with two instructors. They have the firing assemblies. On the signal from the range safety officer, the trainees begin to tie their firing assemblies into the trunk line. These assemblies are similar to the ones used on the previous shots, only they're dual-waterproof firing assemblies. Waterproofing of a nonelectric firing assembly is a technical and highly evolved procedure. During World War II, the Navy expended no small amount of time and money to develop a reliable-waterproof firing assembly. None of them worked.

Early frogmen solved the problem on the job with waterproof neoprene cement, which was used to encase the complete assembly, and two condoms for extra protection from the salt water. They worked every time. Thirty years ago with Class 45, I made waterproof firing assemblies like the World War II frogmen did. Class 228 does it the same way. And the

assemblies still work every time. Class 228's water shot goes high-order, and the class moves on to its final evolution on San Clemente, the field training exercise (FTX).

The FTX is a series of practice combat missions. The class is split into two squads and given different mission scenarios. One is a reconnaissance mission; another is a demolition ambush using claymore mines and automatic weapons. The final exercise is a platoon-size (all 20 trainees), direct-action mission to attack a radar installation. As with the previous two FTX scenarios, the class plans the mission and prepares its equipment by day and goes into the field at night. It's not Hell Week, but the men don't get a lot of sleep during the FTX week. The final night, they come in over the beach, transition to land travel, patrol several miles to the objective area, then slowly and carefully approach the target. With two of the trainees illumi-

The fastest team during Third Phase takes a moment to mug for the camera after their final night assault. This will be considered their graduation picture as a team, although they will be in dress uniforms for a real graduation soon. This has become the appearance they are most comfortable with, and one that they will display many times over the coming months and years. This is the look and dress of Navy SEALs.

nating the target with pop flares, the other trainees assault the target with their M-4 rifles. Once they secure the radar site, they rig key installations and buildings with demolitions.

Time on target is critical, and they must hit and run as SEALs are trained to do. As they patrol away from the objective area, they hear their charges go off, right on schedule. But on the way out, the instructors ambush them with blank ammunition. In a mock battle, the trainees leapfrog away from the "enemy force" and continue on to their beach landing site. There they cross the beach again in tactical order, pull their fins over their boots, and swim for the small inflatable boats they have anchored offshore.

During all the field training exercise problems, the Third Phase staff is watching and grading every

move. When the exercise is over, the tired trainees gather in the classroom for debriefing by the patrol leader and a critique by the instructor in charge of the problem. Each night out they learn, and each subsequent practice mission goes a little smoother. If an evolution is not up to standards, they will go back out and do it again the next night. Class 228 passes all of its FTX missions.

On the final night, the 20 trainees treat the instructors to a barbecue and a keg of beer at the small instructors' lounge at Camp Al Huey. The next day is given over to cleaning up camp and packing gear and weapons for the trip back to Coronado. This is the end of Third Phase and the last hurdle between the men and graduation. Training, but only training at BUD/S, is over for Class 228.

CHAPTER 8
GRADUATION

An officer stands behind the crowd that is gathered for Class 228's graduation from Basic Underwater Demolition/ SEAL (BUD/S) training at the naval amphibious base in Coronado, California.

WEEK

Signifying the start of Class 228's graduation program, the U.S. flag is paraded across the grinder and through the audience at the amphibious base in Coronado. The site of many hours of physical exertion and pain, this is now a place of celebration for the graduates, their friends, and families. The crowd stands in anticipation.

Graduation week, once a dream, is now a reality. It's an easy week, with administrative chores like dental x-rays, jump-school briefings, wet-suit measurements, and course critiques. The commanding officer of the naval special warfare center, as well as the instructor staff, will read these critiques closely. The trainees are out almost every night eating hamburgers, having a beer or two, and celebrating their fellowship. They've made it and they know it.

The last graded physical evolution is the SEAL physical readiness test. It consists of the maximum number of pushups, sit-ups, and dead-hang pull-ups a trainee can do in two-minute intervals. Following the exercises, the men immediately complete a three-mile timed run and a half-mile timed open-ocean swim. There is no punishment for those who finish last, but they're still Basic Underwater Demolition/SEAL (BUD/S) trainees and they fight to be first.

Halfway through its own BUD/S training, Class 229 attends the graduation ceremony. The men will hail the graduating class with a "hoo-yah," which will cost them a trip into the surf and sand. Class 229 attends graduation to pay respect and see that it is possible to make it through the program.

Twenty graduates of the BUD/S training sit at attention awaiting their graduation. They are the best of the men who got "wet and sandy" on their first day of training. Each man is lost in his thoughts, perhaps wondering why he made it and the others failed. However, those family and friends attending the ceremony know. Everyone in the audience knows why these men have made the grade: They are the best of the best.

Retired naval Captain, and co-author of this book, Dick Couch addresses the graduates of Class 228. The months of hard BUD/S training and education have come to a conclusion for these men. They have earned the pride and appreciation of their family and friends who listen in the crowd. Only 10 of the original 114 men in Class 228 remain. Twenty men in all will graduate, the result of medical reassignments from other classes.

Their individual scores will improve when they get to the teams and their bodies recover from the rigors of BUD/S, but they don't do badly. In the allotted time, most of them do more than 100 pushups, more than 150 sit-ups, and in excess of 20 pull-ups. Their run times are in the 15- to 18-minute range.

There are two more physical evolutions between Class 228 and graduation: Hoo-yah physical training and the Balboa Park run. Both evolutions are designed to be fun and to build class spirit prior to graduation. Hoo-yah physical training for Class 228 is a swim-trunks, T-shirts, and boots evolution, but it's not an easy one. The trainees run the O-course, run

seven miles in the soft sand and then run the O-course again. The Balboa Park run is not a competition but an easy jaunt through the palm trees and greenery of the park. It's a team run, a long and easy one.

On Thursday, the members of Class 228 complete their BUD/S checkout, collect their new orders, and rehearse for graduation. At long last, the flags, the rows of folding chairs, and the raised speaker's platform will be for them. On April 21, Class 228 graduates from Basic Underwater Demolition/SEAL training. I have the honor of being their graduation speaker. Like most graduation speakers, I congratulate them on successfully completing this initial and difficult part

BUD/S instructors get a handshake and word of appreciation from a graduate. Then the instructors tell the trainee that they will be proud to serve with him. Despite the fact that the instructors are tough and determined to create a challenging environment for trainees, they are fair and honest in their approach.

Dick Couch, co-author of *To Be a U.S. Navy SEAL*, congratulates the senior officer of Class 228 upon graduation.

of their journey. I also remind them of the hard work ahead—the serious business of learning the professional skills they will need to qualify as Navy SEALs. Then they will begin their SEAL careers as members of an operational SEAL platoon. I remind them that their life as SEAL warriors is one of dedication, attention to detail, and continuous training. They may be finished with BUD/S, but training is never over.

Now that Basic Underwater Demolition/SEAL training is over for Class 228, Class 229 is now the senior class at BUD/S. Its class numerals grace the podium on the BUD/S grinder. It took Class 228 seven months, including the Christmas break and holidays, and a great deal of sweat and pain to get through BUD/S. But the 20 men, 20 BUD/S graduates, are men who still face a great deal more work if they are to qualify as Navy SEALs.

Why did these 20 men make it to this graduation and the other 117 fail? What made 10 of the original 114 who went straight through so unique? I thought a great deal about this as I left BUD/S with Class 228. Certainly, these men embody the Navy's core values of honor, courage, and commitment. But so did many of the men who failed and dropped out. Perhaps the key attribute is some rare, ill-defined personal quality that can only be rendered by a long trial of pain and cold water. Perhaps this is a quality found only in the heart of a warrior. And it's still not over. The odds are that two or three of the BUD/S graduates in Class 228 never will achieve deployment status of being a Navy SEAL. They will find the higher standards of advanced training too difficult. Or once they get their SEAL pin, they may lose their focus or be unable to maintain commitment to the excellence required of

A Navy SEAL earns his trident pin after more than a year of extensive and intensive basic training. The trident identifies a SEAL in much the same manner as flight wings do a pilot. Even with all of this basic training, this young SEAL's training will start all over again upon assignment to an active team. Active-duty SEALs spend their entire careers training and improving previously learned skills.

Navy SEALs. They may be surprised that it never gets any easier, that the life of a warrior is a never-ending one of sacrifice and continuous training.

I did learn something of Class 228 when I met the graduates' parents. Uniformly, they were men and women who had high expectations of their sons, parents who set goals and subscribed to a strong work ethic. I sensed there was a commitment to personal and family values in the home. It was difficult to tell who was prouder—the parents or the graduates—but few of the parents were surprised that their son made it through BUD/S. They expected it and were simply delighted to attend the graduation and share in their son's accomplishment.

I personally have come to believe the single trait that will get a man through BUD/S is the will to win. The desire to win is different from refusing to lose or not quitting. If he can meet the performance standards, a man can get through BUD/S by refusing to

quit, but he will not be a leader or a "go-to" guy in his SEAL platoon. BUD/S cultivates this will to win, but to one degree or another top trainees bring it with them when they walk through the door of the naval special warfare center. Some realize this only after they leave BUD/S.

When a man graduates from BUD/S, the real professional SEAL training begins. After Army Airborne training or "jump school," he must successfully complete SEAL qualification training (SQT) to earn his SEAL pin. Then he joins a SEAL platoon and begins 18 months of intensive training to prepare for operational deployment.

The men of Class 228 are now on the job. They are SEALs and serving in operational SEAL platoons around the world. It is these fine young men, and their brother SEALs, who will carry the fight against Al Qaeda terrorism or anyone else who threatens our nation.

Cliff Hollenbeck (LEFT)

Cliff Hollenbeck is a leading international photographer, film producer, and composer. He is the author of more than a dozen best-selling books on photography, travel, and business, including the pictorial book *Mexico*, with introduction by James A. Michener. He has also written two novels involving former Navy SEALs as characters. Cliff has twice been named "Travel Photographer of the Year" by the Society of American Travel Writers. His film company has received gold medals at the New York and Chicago Film Festivals and Tellys for several travel commercials and travel videos. He has released two CDs of Italian arias. His clients include international airlines, cruise lines, advertising agencies, magazines, and book publishers. He spent six years in the Navy during the Vietnam era, including three years as a photojournalist with special warfare groups. Cliff and his wife Nancy live in Washington state. He is a member of the UDT-SEAL Association.

Dick Couch (RIGHT)

Dick Couch is one of the leading authors on the subject of special operations. He has written four successful novels, including best-sellers *SEAL Team One* and *Rising Wind*, and two nonfiction books on SEAL team training, *The Warrior Elite* and *The Finishing School*. *The Finishing School*, which follows Basic Underwater Demolition/SEAL graduates as they complete their SEAL qualification and become ready to join a combat-capable platoon, is scheduled for publication in November 2003. Dick is a graduate of the U.S. Naval Academy and was the honor man from SEAL team training Class 45. As a platoon commander with SEAL Team One, he led one of the few successful POW rescue operations of the Vietnam War. Following his service in the Navy, he served with the Central Intelligence Agency as a maritime operations officer. Dick retired from the Naval Reserve in 1997 as the senior reserve SEAL officer, with the rank of captain. He is a sought-after motivational speaker and frequently appears as a commentator on national TV and radio. Dick and his wife Julia live in Ketchum, Idaho. He is a member of the UDT-SEAL Association.

INDEX

To Be a U.S. Army Ranger
ISBN 0-7603-1314-8

Conflict Iraq
ISBN 0-7603-1592-2

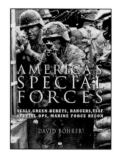

America's Special Forces
ISBN 0-7603-1348-2

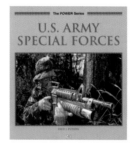

U.S. Army Special Forces
ISBN 0-7603-0862-4

U.S. Air Force Special Ops
ISBN 0-7603-0733-4

**Illustrated Directory of
Special Forces**
ISBN 0-7603-1419-5

Special Ops
ISBN 0-7603-1603-1